100
Bible
Math
Mistakes

Robert Collins

This book is dedicated to
Pat Cleveland,
friend and inspiration

Freethinker's Books™, LLC
Birmingham, Alabama, USA

www.freethinkersbooks.com

ISBN 9780-615-38173-2

Contents

Introduction   i

Chapter 1 - Jesus' Math Mistakes   1

Chapter 2 - Math Mistakes About Jesus   26

Chapter 3 - Historical Math Mistakes   44

Chapter 4 - Sexual Math Mistakes   73

Chapter 5 - Theological Math Mistakes   81

Chapter 6 - Scientific and Geometrical Math Mistakes   98

Notes   111

Appendix 1 - Jesus Paid For Everyone's Sins With 1 Bad Day   114

Appendix 2 - Blind Faith   116

Index Of Bible References   117

Subject Index   130

Introduction

"Prove all things" - 1 Thessalonians 5:21

"Numbers don't lie" - Common saying

Is the Bible the Word of God? Generations of Bible scholars have tried to prove this with millions of hours of study in archeology, textual analysis and apologetics. The answer is simple and can be determined from the Bible itself.

The vast majority of people, including yourself, already know how to determine whether a document, person or organization is trustworthy. We make these decisions every time we sign a contract, enter into a long-term relationship, make a major purchase, watch a newscast or undergo a medical procedure. How do we decide who or what we can trust?

We all know that truth and accuracy are habits, and so are error or deceit. A person or document that is trustworthy about things that we can verify is more likely to be trustworthy about things that we cannot verify. Likewise, someone or something that makes statements that we can prove are mistaken or misleading is likely to have the same problem with statements that we cannot prove or disprove. In fact, if a source of information is unreliable enough, just about all of us will decide not to believe it at all.

The Bible makes many claims that are unverifiable and can be accepted only by faith. But the Bible makes many other claims that can easily be verified. Many of these are mathematical and can be quickly proven or disproven, usually without even a pocket calculator.

Occasional mathematical errors may be attributed to sloppy copyists. Although this raises the question of why God would inspire perfect originals but would not inspire perfect copies, it does leave a bit of room for those who have faith that all apparent mistakes will someday be resolved.

But if the Bible contains large numbers of mathematical errors, it becomes impossible to believe that the Bible is a trustworthy book. This is particularly true if many of these errors are supported by a wide variety of manuscripts and translations, and/or are so integral to the text that it is unlikely they were caused by incompetent copying.

If the Bible's "God Almighty" was so sloppy as to repeatedly get his numbers wrong, then whoever wrote the Bible is neither God nor Almighty and the Bible is simply a collection of myths that is no more truthful than the mathematical errors it contains.

Chapter 1

Jesus' Math Mistakes

If there was ever a man who should have always gotten his numbers right, it would have to be Jesus Christ:

• Jesus claimed to be God in John 14:9, "He that hath seen me hath seen the Father". So did his biographers in John 1:1, "The Word was God" and Colossians 2:9, "In him dwelleth all the fullness of the God-head bodily".

• Jesus claimed to be omnipotent, "All power is given unto me in heaven and in earth", Matthew 28:18.

• The Bible says that Jesus created everything in the entire universe, which would have included all of the laws of physics and mathematics, "All things were made by him; and without him was not any thing made that was made", John 1:3.

• Since Jesus believed himself to be God, he believed he was perfect and demanded perfection of his followers, "Be ye therefore perfect, even as your Father which is in heaven is perfect", Matthew 5:48

• Jesus even claimed to maintain a continually-updated database of detailed mathematical information about his followers, "The very hairs of your head are all numbered", Matthew 10:30, Luke 12:7

If the Bible is historically truthful, however, Jesus was dogmatically confident but woefully inaccurate even when discussing simple numbers like 1, 2, 3 and 12. Geometrical concepts understood by every 21st century grade-school student were unknown to him. Any computer programmer or accountant who was that careless with their numbers would quickly be fired.

Nevertheless, Jesus claims to be building the universe's largest database and plans to use it to judge billions of people, "I saw the dead, small and great, stand before God; and the books were opened: and another book was opened, which is the book of life: and the dead were judged out of those things which were written in the books, according to their works ... And whosoever was not found written in the book of life was cast into the lake of fire", Revelation 20:12-15.

Despite his incompetence with numbers, Jesus did alright for himself. Two thousand years later, millions of people are still giving him ten percent of their income. This explains why Christian conservative areas of the world lag behind many other regions in public support for education, particularly in the areas of science and math. If Jesus didn't need it, neither do they.

Jesus Was Wrong About His Own Resurrection

In Matthew 12:40, Jesus said, "As Jonas [Jonah] was three days and three nights in the whale's belly, so shall the Son of Man be three days and three nights in the heart of the earth". This is a reference to Jonah 1:17, "Jonah was in the belly of the fish three days and three nights". This prophecy, which is repeated in Matthew 16:4 and Luke 11:29-30, is a very precise prophecy from the lips of Jesus himself, and it is demonstrably false from the Bible itself.

The Gospels make very definite statements that Jesus died on a Friday afternoon and was raised around dawn on the following Sunday morning. This belief is foundational to Christian theology and is the basis for Good Friday and Easter Sunday rituals celebrated every year.

From Friday afternoon to Sunday morning is at most 40 hours, not three days and nights. Although it is stretching the facts, some will argue this did include portions of three days, since Jewish days are counted from sundown to sundown.

However, there is just no way to get "three nights" out of this. Mark 15:37-47, Luke 23:46-56 and John 19:31-42 all say that Jesus died on Friday shortly before the Sabbath, which began at sundown. Matthew 28:1-7, Mark 16:1-6, Luke 24:1-6, and John 20:1 all say that Jesus was raised around sunrise on Sunday morning. Friday afternoon to Sunday morning is **two** nights.

Jesus prophesied falsely about the most important event in Christian theology: his own resurrection. According to the book of Deuteronomy, this makes Jesus a false prophet. Deuteronomy 18:22 says, "When a prophet speaketh in the name of the Lord, if the thing follow not, nor come to pass, that is the thing which the Lord hath not spoken". If Jesus said something that God did not say, he cannot be God.

Christians themselves cannot agree about how to calculate the date for Easter, supposedly the day of the resurrection. Protestant and Catholic Christians use the Gregorian calendar. Eastern Orthodox and Coptic Christians use the Julian calendar. The result is that they disagree more often than not. During the years 1982-2009, eastern and western Christians celebrated Easter on the same day only 6 times, i.e., less than 1/4 of the time. The Bible claims that Jesus' resurrection occurred on the Sunday after the Jewish Passover holiday, which occurs on the 14th day of the month of Nisan as required by Leviticus 23:5. But many Christians' calculations of Easter are so different from the Jewish calculation of Passover that they sometimes disagree by several weeks.

Jesus Was Wrong Again About His Own Resurrection

In Luke 23:43 Jesus said to one of the thieves who was crucified with him, "Verily I say unto thee, To day shalt thou be with me in paradise". Although the Bible says nothing to contradict the belief that the thief went to paradise on that day, the Bible says twice that Jesus did not go to paradise until at least two or three days later.

Before his crucifixion, Jesus clearly said that he would not go to Heaven until three days after he died. Matthew 12:39-40 says, "He [Jesus] ... said unto them, As Jonas [Jonah] was three days and three nights in the whale's belly, so shall the Son of Man be three days and three nights in the heart of the earth". Variations of this statement are repeated in Matthew 16:4 and Luke 11:29-30. This is such an important Christian belief that one of the most widely accepted statements of faith, The Apostles' Creed, says, "He [Jesus] suffered under Pontius Pilate, was crucified, died, and was buried. He descended into hell".

Shortly after Jesus raised from the dead, the Bible makes it equally clear that he had not been to Paradise since being crucified. On the Sunday morning of his resurrection, Jesus told Mary Magdalene, "Touch me not; for I am not yet ascended to my Father," in John 20:17. Apparently Jesus did go to his father sometime afterwards, because he allowed himself to be touched in John 20:27.

Some apologists point out that ancient Greek did not have punctuation and claim that Luke 23:43 has been mistranslated, that the comma should be placed after "today" not before. They claim that Jesus really said, "Verily I say unto thee today, thou shalt be with me in paradise". In other words, Jesus didn't say he would be in Paradise "today", he merely said he was speaking today. This interpretation is in the New World Translation, which is used by Jehovah's Witnesses. There are three very good reasons why this interpretation is invalid.

The first reason is that a very large number of well-respected modern translations agree with the King James Bible's punctuation of Luke 23:43. These include the New American Standard, American Standard, Revised Standard, New International, Rheims, New King James, Good News Bible, and many others.

The second reason is that Jesus used the phrase "Verily I say unto thee" or "Verily I say unto you", eight times in the Gospel of Luke - Luke 4:24, 11:51, 12:37, 13:35, 18:17, 18:29 21:32 and 23:43. None of these include "today" except Luke 23:43.

Third, "Verily I say unto thee today" does not make grammatical sense. Of course he was saying that "today". When else would he be saying it? He couldn't have recorded it on a digital recorder.

Will The 2,000 Year Old Guy Please Show Himself?

In Matthew 16:28, Jesus said, "Verily I say unto you, There be some standing here, which shall not taste of death, till they see the Son of man coming in his kingdom". In Luke 9:27, Jesus said, "I tell you of a truth, there be some standing here, which shall not taste of death, till they see the kingdom of God".

The verses immediately preceding these verses make it very clear that Jesus was talking about the Judgement Day. Matthew 16:27 says, "The Son of man shall come in the glory of his Father with his angels; and then he shall reward every man according to his works". Luke 9:26 says, "Whosoever shall be ashamed of me and of my words, of him shall the Son of man be ashamed, when he shall come in his own glory, and in his Father's, and of the holy angels".

Jesus' followers certainly believed that he would come back in their lifetimes. Acts 2:44-45 says, "All that believed were together, and had all things common, and sold their possessions and goods, and parted them to all men, as every man had need". 1 Corinthians 7:29 says, "This I say, brethren, the time is short, it remaineth, that ... they that have wives be as though they had none". Few people are going to give up all of their possessions and even their wife unless they think the end is very near.

Of course, Jesus didn't come back when he said he would. The Christians who gave away all of their possessions became "the poor saints which are at Jerusalem", mentioned in Romans 15:26.

Ancient and medieval theologians simply couldn't believe that Matthew 16:28 and Luke 9:27 were wrong, even when interpreted very literally. So the story of the "Wandering Jew" evolved. This man was supposedly present when Jesus spoke these words and was incapable of dying until Jesus returned. He was described as a shoemaker, doorman at Pilate's house or a Roman guard, and was given various names such as Cartaphilus, Longinus, Ahasver, John Buttadaeus, Isaac Laquedem, Count St Germain, Malchus or Joseph of Arimathea. This belief was supported by numerous confirmed sightings in Armenia, Germany, Spain, France, Austria and Italy. Credible witnesses included many French nobles and an Armenian archbishop who reported that he had talked with Cartaphilus, who was now a Christian.

In medieval times, the existence of a living man who had actually spoken with Jesus was widely accepted as powerful evidence in support of Christianity. If this 2,000 year old man would please step forward and let me verify his age by carbon-14 dating a sample of his brain stem at my own expense, I will gladly remove this paragraph from future editions of this book.

1 Body - (1 Hand + 1 Foot + 1 Eye + 1 Private Part) = Salvation

In Matthew 18:8-9, Jesus said,"Wherefore if thy hand or thy foot offend thee, cut them off, and cast them from thee, it is better for thee to enter into life halt or maimed, rather than having two hands or two feet to be cast into everlasting fire. And if thine eye offend thee, pluck it out, and cast it from thee, it is better for thee to enter into life with one eye, rather than having two eyes to be cast into hell fire". This idea is repeated in Matthew 5:29-30 and Mark 9:43-48.

This admonishment was not limited to hands, feet and eyes. In Matthew 19:12, Jesus said, "There be eunuchs, which have made themselves eunuchs for the kingdom of heaven's sake". A eunuch is a man whose testicles have been removed.

These verses were taken very literally by some early Christians, who were so worried about sexual sins that they literally cut off their temptation. Saint Origen of Alexandria[1] and Bishop Melito of Sardis believed that Jesus' advice provided the perfect solution for the problem of lust, so they had themselves castrated. This occasionally happens in modern times. Boston Corbett had a "born again" experience and soon thereafter, in 1858, castrated himself with a pair of scissors. (Corbett later served with the Union army in the United States' Civil War and earned his place in history by killing John Wilkes Booth, the man who had assassinated President Lincoln.)

This literal application of these passages in Matthew and Mark have never been very popular among Bible believers. I can't imagine why.

These verses did, however, solve a serious problem for many Medieval and Renaissance churches. 1 Corinthians 14:34-35 says, "Let your women keep silence in the churches, for it is not permitted unto them to speak ... it is a shame for women to speak in the church". So where was the church choir going to find singers who could hit the high notes? The solution was "Castrato Tenors". Churches would find musically talented young boys and castrate them "for the kingdom of heaven's sake" so that their voices would not become deeper when they reached puberty.

The church eventually outlawed religious castration because procreation is the most effective way to make more church members. Perhaps this quaint doctrine should be revived as part of a rehabilitation program for deviant priests and ministers in Christian denominations where pedophilia by their own professionals has been a tradition almost as long-standing and prevalent as Communion.

Jesus, The Devil And A Flat Earth

Luke 4:5-7 says, "The Devil, taking him [Jesus] up into an high mountain, shewed unto him all the kingdoms of the world **in a moment of time**. And the devil said unto him, All this power will I give thee and the glory of them, for that is delivered unto me; and to whomsoever I will I give it. If thou therefore wilt worship me".

It is impossible to see "all the kingdoms of the world in a moment of time" because the Earth is a sphere. Even if Jesus' "high mountain" was on the moon, there is no way to see the Roman, Persian, Indian, Chinese, African and American kingdoms "in a moment of time" on a spherical Earth. But if you believe that the earth is flat or only slightly curved, it is easy to believe that there is a mountain somewhere that is tall enough to see all of it.

This obvious error is made even more embarrassing by the fact that Greek and Roman scientists had known that the Earth was spherical for over a century before New Testament times. Eratosthenes had calculated its circumference as 25,000 miles, very close to the modern figures of 24,859 (polar) or 24,891 (equatorial) miles.

When you tell Bible believers about Luke 4:5, they usually say that Jesus merely had a vision, so the mountain did not really have to exist. There are two very serious problems with this interpretation.

First, the surrounding verses, Luke 4:1-13, very strongly argue in favor of the text claiming to be literal history, not a vision..

• Luke says that Jesus, "Being forty days tempted of the devil. And in those days he did eat nothing: and when they were ended, he afterward hungered". 40 days of starvation constituted a substantial assault to a person's will power. Having a vision of fasting for 40 days is meaningless.

• Luke and Matthew both report that the Devil tempted Jesus to change stones into bread. If you had literally fasted for 40 days and turned down the temptation to eat bread, it would be powerful evidence of resisting temptation. If it was merely a vision, it loses its value.

• Luke and Matthew both say that the Devil set Jesus on "a pinnacle of the temple", i.e., the Jewish temple in Jerusalem, and tempted him to jump off and let angels save him. This can only be significant if jumping off would have put Jesus in very real physical danger.

Second, assuming that Luke 4:5-7 is merely a vision casts doubt on one of Christianity's most important doctrines: the belief that Jesus can help believers resist temptation because he has been tempted himself, as reported in Hebrews 4:15, "We have not an high priest which cannot be touched with the feeling of our infirmities, but was in all points tempted like as we are, yet without sin". If the mountain was imaginary, the temptation was too.

Not All That Take The Sword Shall Perish With The Sword

One of Jesus' more famous sayings is in Matthew 26:52, "**All** they that take the sword shall perish with the sword". Although Jesus' words were ignored by his followers who started Crusades and other holy wars, most Christian priests and ministers scrupulously heeded Jesus' admonition, which is why the church settled many theological disputes by bloodlessly hanging, drowning, crushing or burning dissenters.

The Bible itself proves that Jesus' statement is false, because it says that many people who "took the sword" died peacefully.

In Exodus 32:27-28, Moses commanded that the Israelites, "slay every man his brother, and every man his companion, and every man his neighbour", killing about 3,000 Israelites. In Numbers 21:3 they, "utterly destroyed them [Hormah] and their cities". In Numbers 21:33-35, "They smote ... all his people [Bashan], until there was none left alive" in 60 cities and "a great many unwalled towns". In Numbers 31:6-35, Moses ordered the murders of tens of thousands of Midianite boys and women. Yet Moses died peacefully and angels buried him, according to Deuteronomy 34:1-6 and Jude 1:9.

The Israelite army under Joshua's command "smote with the sword" millions of non-Israelites. This is detailed in "God Ordered > 3,000,000 Violations Of 'Thou Shalt Not Murder'" on page 54 of this book. Yet Joshua 24:29 says that he died peacefully at the age of 110.

King "David and his men went up, and invaded the Geshurites and the Gezrites ... David smote the land, and left neither man nor woman alive", according to 1 Samuel 27:9. In 2 Samuel 5:7-9, he said, "Whosoever ... smiteth ... the lame and the blind ... he shall be chief and captain". David murdered Uriah the Hittite in 2 Samuel chapters 11-12. David killed so many people that God told him, "Thou hast shed blood abundantly, and hast made great wars, thou shalt not build an house unto my name, because thou hast shed much blood upon the earth in my sight" in 1 Chronicles 22:8. Yet 1 Kings chapters 1-2 says that David died at a ripe old age while a "fair damsel" kept him warm.

2 Kings 10:16-36 reports that, because of King Jehu's "zeal for the Lord", "he slew all that remained unto Ahab in Samaria". Then, "The Lord said unto Jehu, Because thou hast done well in executing that which is right in Mine eyes, and hast done unto the house of Ahab according to all that was in Mine heart, thy children of the fourth generation shall sit on the throne of Israel". The Bible says that Jehu had a long reign of 28 years and "slept with his fathers".

If Jesus did not really mean it when he said, "All they that take the sword shall perish with the sword", it has profound theological implications. For more information, please refer to "All Is Not All" on page 92 of this book.

How Many Times, And When, Did The Cock Crow?

The story of Peter's denial is so important that it is reported in all 4 Gospels. Each one starts with Jesus' prediction that Peter will deny knowing him. Matthew 26:34 says, "Jesus said unto him [Peter], Verily I say unto thee, That this night, before the cock crow, thou shalt deny me thrice". This is similar to Luke 22:34, "I tell thee, Peter, the cock shall not crow this day, before that thou shalt thrice deny that thou knowest me", and John 13:38, "Verily, verily, I say unto thee, The cock shall not crow, till thou hast denied me thrice".

Matthew, Luke and John sync up fairly well:

• Denial #1: "Peter sat without in the palace: and a damsel came unto him, saying, Thou also wast with Jesus of Galilee. But he denied before them all, saying, I know not what thou sayest", Matthew 26:69-70, see also Luke 22:56-57 and John 18:17

• Denial #2: "When he was gone out into the porch, another maid saw him, and said unto them that were there, This fellow was also with Jesus of Nazareth. And again he denied with an oath, I do not know the man", Matthew 26:71-72, see also Luke 22:58 and John 18:25

• Denial #3: "After a while came unto him they that stood by, and said to Peter, Surely thou also art one of them; for thy speech bewrayeth thee. Then began he to curse and to swear, saying, I know not the man", Matthew 26:73-74, Luke 22:59-60 and John 18:26

• Cock Crows: "Immediately the cock crew", Matthew 26:74, Luke 22:60 and John 18:27

But the Gospel of Mark tells it differently. Mark 14:30 says, "Verily I [Jesus] say unto thee, That this day, even in this night, before the cock crow twice, thou shalt deny me thrice".

• Denial #1: "When she saw Peter warming himself, she looked upon him, and said, And thou also wast with Jesus of Nazareth. But he denied, saying, I know not, neither understand I what thou sayest", Mark 14:67-68

• Cock's Crow #1: "The cock crew", Mark 14:68

• Denial #2: "A maid saw him again, and began to say to them that stood by, This is one of them. And he denied it again", Mark 14:69-70

• Denial #3: "A little after, they that stood by said again to Peter, Surely thou art one of them: for thou art a Galilaean, and thy speech agreeth thereto. But he began to curse and to swear, saying, I know not this man of whom ye speak", Mark 14:70-71.

• Cock's Crow #2: "the second time the cock crew" Mark 14:72

Jesus Will Be Short 1 Judge On The Judgement Day

In Matthew 19:28, Jesus told his Apostles, "Ye also shall sit upon twelve thrones, judging the twelve tribes of Israel", i.e., one throne for each of the them.

The author of Matthew tells us exactly who these twelve Apostles were. According to Matthew 10:2-4, "The names of the twelve Apostles are these: The first, Simon, who is called Peter, and Andrew his brother, James the son of Zebedee and John his brother, Philip, and Bartholomew, Thomas and Matthew the publican, James the son of Alphaeus, and Lebbaeus, whose surname was Thaddaeus, Simon the Canaanite, and Judas Iscariot, who also betrayed him."

Many Bible passages confirm the claim that Judas Iscariot was one of the twelve apostles, including Matthew 26:14, 26:47, Mark 14:10, 14:18-20, 14:43, Luke 22:3, 22:47, and John 7:70-71. But Judas will not be sitting on any thrones or judging anyone on the Judgement Day. Judas betrayed Jesus and, "It had been good for that man if he had not been born," according to Matthew 26:24. Judas is the "son of perdition" who is "lost", according to John 17:12. He will be burning in Hell on the Judgement Day, if the Bible is true.

This means that Jesus' prophecy in Matthew 19:28 is short by 1. The Bible says that eleven of the Apostles will get a throne, but Judas will not. Jesus surely knew better than to promise a throne to Judas. "Jesus knew from the beginning who they were that believed not, and who should betray him ... 'Have not I chosen you twelve, and one of you is a devil?' He spake of Judas Iscariot the son of Simon, for he it was that should betray him, being one of the twelve." John 6:64-71.

Jesus is a false prophet according to Deuteronomy 18:22, "When a prophet speaketh in the name of the Lord, if the thing follow not, nor come to pass, that is the thing which the Lord hath not spoken, but the prophet hath spoken it presumptuously: thou shalt not be afraid of him". Note that there is no margin of error. It doesn't say "close", "almost" or "round up to an even number". If a prophecy does not happen exactly the way the prophet predicts it will, he is a false prophet. According to Deuteronomy 18:20, "The prophet which shall presume to speak a word in my [God's] name, which I have not commanded him to speak ... even that prophet shall die."

The importance of this mathematical misstatement cannot be overestimated. Jesus falsely predicted who was going to be doing the judging on the Judgement Day. Belief in the Judgement Day is one of the most important doctrines of conservative Christianity. God, if he exists, certainly knows everything, which includes knowing who is going to be doing the judging on the Judgement Day. If Jesus really made this mistake, either he cannot be God or God doesn't know everything. If God doesn't know everything, he is not God.

1 ≠ **Many**

Matthew 12:38-40 says, "Then certain of the scribes and of the Pharisees answered, saying, Master, we would see a sign from thee. But he [Jesus] answered and said unto them, An evil and adulterous generation seeketh after a sign; and there shall no sign be given to it, but the sign of the prophet Jonas [Jonah] For as Jonas was three days and three nights in the whale's belly; so shall the Son of man be three days and three nights in the heart of the earth."

This is such an important statement that parts of it are repeated in Matthew 16:4 and Luke 11:29.

Mark 8:11-12 is even more dogmatic, claiming that Jesus said he would give no sign at all, "The Pharisees came forth and began to question with him, seeking of him a sign from heaven, tempting him. And he sighed deeply in his spirit, and saith, Why doth this generation seek after a sign? Verily I say unto you, there shall no sign be given unto this generation."

If these passages are accurate, Jesus would have performed no more than one "sign", i.e., "the sign of the prophet Jonas", his resurrection. But the Gospel of John, as well as the books of Acts and Hebrews, say that Jesus performed many signs. The Greek word translated "sign" in Matthew 12:38-40, Matthew 16:4, Mark 8:11-13 and Luke 11:29 is "semeion".

Some apologists argue that Jesus was saying that only the "evil generation" would not see any signs. But the Bible very clearly says that Jesus signs were seen by many different groups of people, including unbelieving Jews and even the unrepentant Jewish leaders involved in Jesus' crucifixion.

Many of Jesus' signs were seen by unbelievers:

• Acts 2:22-23, "Ye men of Israel, hear these words; Jesus of Nazareth, a man approved of God among you by miracles and wonders and signs [semeion], which God did by him in the midst of you, as ye yourselves also know him, being delivered by the determinate counsel and foreknowledge of God, ye have taken, and by wicked hands have crucified and slain". Note that the speaker specifically told unbelieving Jews that there had been, "signs [semeion], which God did by him [Jesus] in the midst of you". These were the same Jews who, "Him [Jesus] ... ye have taken, and by wicked hands have crucified and slain".

• John 6:26, "Ye seek me [Jesus], not because ye saw the miracles [semeion], but because ye did eat of the loaves, and were filled".

• John 12:37, "Though he [Jesus] had done so many miracles [semeion] before them, yet they believed not on him"

(continued on the next page)

Many people saw the signs:

• John 6:2 "a great multitude followed him [Jesus], because they saw his miracles [semeion]"

• John 6:14, "Then those men, when they had seen the miracle [semeion] that Jesus did, said, This is of a truth that prophet"

• John 12:17-18 says, "The people therefore that were with him [Jesus] when he called Lazarus out of his grave, and raised him from the dead, bare record. For this cause the people also met him, for that they heard that he had done this miracle [semeion]"

Many people believed in Jesus because of the signs:

• John 2:23, "Many believed in his name, when they saw the miracles [semeion] which he did

• John 3:2, "Rabbi , we know that thou art a teacher come from God, for no man can do these miracles [semeion] that thou doest, except God be with him"

• John 4:48-54, "Then said Jesus unto him, Except ye see signs [semeion] and wonders, ye will not believe. The nobleman saith unto him, Sir, come down ere my child die ... Jesus saith unto him, Go thy way; thy son liveth. And the man believed the word that Jesus had spoken unto him ... his servants met him, and told him, saying, Thy son liveth ... So the father knew that it was at the same hour, in the which Jesus said unto him, Thy son liveth: and himself believed, and his whole house. This is again the second miracle [semeion] that Jesus did."

• John 7:31, "Many of the people believed on him, and said, When Christ cometh, will he do more miracles [semeion] than these which this man hath done?"

• John 10:41-42, "Many resorted unto him, and said, John [the Baptist] did no miracle [semeion], but all things that John spake of this man were true, And many believed on him there."

• John 11:45 says that after Jesus raised Lazarus from the dead, "many of the Jews which came to Mary [Lazarus' sister], and had seen the things which Jesus did, believed on him".

Jesus performed many other signs:

• John 20:30, "many other signs [semeion] truly did Jesus in the presence of his disciples, which are not written in this book".

• Hebrews 2:3-4 says, "so great salvation; which at the first began to be spoken by the Lord, and was confirmed unto us by them that heard him; God also bearing them witness, both with signs and wonders, and with divers miracles". The Greek word translated "signs" in Hebrews 2:4 is "semeiois", which is the plural of "semeion".

0 Temptations ≠ Many Temptations

The Bible is very clear when it claims that God does not tempt anyone. James 1:13 says "Let no man say when he is tempted, I am tempted of God, for God ... neither tempteth he any man". One of the most famous passages in the Bible is "The Lord's Prayer", in Matthew chapter 6, where Jesus said, "Lead us not into temptation, but deliver us from evil".

But the Bible says quite clearly that Jesus did tempt at least one person, in John 6:5-6, "When Jesus then lifted up his eyes, and saw a great company come unto him, he saith unto Philip, Whence shall we buy bread, that these may eat? And this he said to prove him: for he himself knew what he would do". The Greek word translated "prove" in this passage is "peirazo". It is the same word translated "tempt" three times in James 1:13 (see above), which says that God never tempts anyone.

Sometimes God and Jesus did more than merely tempt someone. They actually caused people to sin.

Jesus created an inescapable sin in Matthew 5:32, "Whosoever shall put away his wife, saving for the cause of fornication, causeth her to commit adultery". According to Jesus, a woman who is completely faithful to her husband becomes an adulteress when he divorces her even when it is not her fault. She has no choice.

Not to be outdone, Jesus' dad, Jehovah, created many inescapable sins in the Old Testament. Genesis 22:1 says, "God did tempt Abraham" by telling him to sacrifice his son Isaac. But this was more than a temptation. It was an inescapable sin. Abraham could emotionally abuse his son by tying him to an altar and preparing to sacrifice him, or he could disobey a direct command from God. Another inescapable sin is reported in 2 Samuel chapter 24, which says that God, "moved David ... to say, Go, number Israel and Judah", then God killed 70,000 Hebrews because David did what God moved him to do.

Even these bizarre stories pale beside the inescapable sins that God created for the Israelites when he repeatedly commanded them to commit mass murder. Examples include Deuteronomy 20:16-17, "Thou shalt save alive nothing that breatheth, But thou shalt utterly destroy them; namely, the Hittites, and the Amorites, the Canaanites, and the Perizzites, the Hivites, and the Jebusites; as the Lord thy God hath commanded thee", and 1 Samuel 15:3, "Utterly destroy all that they have, and spare them not, but slay both man and woman, infant and suckling". The Israelites had to choose between disobeying one of God's Ten Commandments, "Thou shalt not kill", or disobeying God's direct order to murder millions of women and children.

Most bizarre and cruel of all, however, is God's statement in Jeremiah 19:9, "I will cause them to eat the flesh of their sons and the flesh of their daughters", a threat which God fulfilled in Lamentations 2:20 and 4:10.

Over 100 Gallons Of Tasty Temptation To Sin

John 2:1-11 describes the miracle of Jesus changing the water to wine at the wedding in Cana in Galilee. This was a lot of wine, so much that it filled 6 water pots. The King James says that each water pot could hold "two or three firkins apiece". A "firkin" is about 1/4 of a barrel. A barrel is about 31 gallons, so a firkin is about 8 gallons; each pot held 16-24 gallons. Many modern translations say that each pot held "about 20 gallons" or something similar. 20 gallons * 6 pots = 120 gallons of wine.

That is equivalent to about 450 one-liter bottles of wine. Many people can get knee-walking toilet-hugging drunk on a liter of wine; this was even more true in ancient times because people were physically smaller (see "Biostatistics vs. Jesus" on page 17 of this book). Note also that, in John 2:10, one of the guests observed that the men at the party already "have well drunk", so much so that they had consumed all of the wine their host had available.

Drunkenness is a sin. Ephesians 5:18 commands, "Be not drunk with wine". Proverbs 23:29-32 says, "Who hath woe? Who hath sorrow? Who hath contentions? Who hath babbling? Who hath wounds without cause? Who hath redness of eyes? They that tarry long at the wine, they that go to seek mixed wine. Look not thou upon the wine when it is red, when it giveth his colour in the cup, when it moveth itself aright. At the last it biteth like a serpent, and stingeth like an adder".

Giving over a hundred gallons of additional wine to a bunch of people who had already imbibed freely constituted a temptation to become drunk. To make matters worse, John 2:10 says that the wine that Jesus miraculously created was much tastier than the wine that the guests had already consumed, enhancing the temptation.

But James 1:13 says "Let no man say when he is tempted, I am tempted of God: for God ... neither tempteth he any man".

Bible believers usually try to explain this by saying that it was not really wine; it was non-alcoholic grape juice. This ignores this passage's clear statements that Jesus changed the water into wine. This was confirmed by "ruler of the feast", equivalent to a modern head waiter or wine steward, who tasted it and told the bridegroom, "thou hast kept the good wine until now" in John 2:9-10. It is easy to tell the difference between wine and grape juice. Just taste it. I have reviewed dozens of Bible translations and cannot find a single one that says "grape juice". They all say "wine".

The Greek word repeateldly used and translated "wine" in John 2:1-11 is "oinos". It is the same word used in Ephesians 5:18, "be not drunk with wine [oinos]". Other passages are equally clear. 1 Timothy 3:8 says, "Likewise must the deacons be ... not given to much wine [oinos]". Titus 2:3 says, "The aged women likewise, that they be in behaviour as becometh holiness ... not given to much wine [oinos]".

(1 Praying Little Old Lady) * 2 = No Need For Hospitals

In Matthew 18:19-20, Jesus said, "I say unto you, if two of you shall agree on earth as touching any thing that they shall ask, it shall be done for them of my Father which is in heaven. For where two or three are gathered in my name, there I am in the midst of them". This is a common claim in the Bible. Matthew 21:22 says, "All things, whatsoever ye shall ask in prayer, believing, ye shall receive". John 14:13-14 says, "Whatsoever ye shall ask in my name, that will I do ... If ye shall ask any thing in my name, I will do it". See also John 15:7 and 15:16.

These are some of the most demonstrably false passages in the Bible. If these verses were true, Christian hospitals would cure people at higher rates than similarly equipped/staffed non-Christian hospitals, but they don't. This would not be a subtle effect, it would be profound because God himself would be healing people. Hospital care in the United States is highly competitive; hospitals often try to gain a competitive advantage by advertising that they are superior in trained staff, certifications and/or technology. But no Christian hospital dares to advertise, "We heal our patients better than the Jewish hospital across the street" or "Our doctors get better results because they pray for their patients". If they tried to do so, competing hospitals would immediately sue them for false advertising.

If these verses were true, populations with a high percentage of Christians should be healthier than populations with a lower percentage of Christians. Much of modern Europe can be accurately described as "post-Christian". But the Medieval Christian ancestors of modern Europeans lived, on average, only a third as long as Europeans do today. Atheism is on the rise in all of the modern world and so is longevity. If Matthew 18:19-20 is true, we would see the exact opposite of what is happening to the lifespans of hundreds of millions of people.

If these verses were true, ambulances would not need paramedics and hospitals would not need doctors or medicines. All they would need would be two or three little old ladies who were right with Jesus, agreed with each other and liked to pray.

Christians try to wiggle out of this by saying that Jesus always answers prayers, but sometimes Jesus' answer is not "yes"; it is "wait", "something different" or "no". There are two fatal flaws with this argument.

First, that is nowhere close to what the Bible says. The Bible says that Jesus explicitly said, "it shall be done for them", not "something different", not "no", and if the prayer needs a quick response (like when Granny has a heart attack), not "wait".

Second, no matter who/what you pray to, whether it is Jesus, Mithra, Zeus, your deceased ancestors or no one at all, one of those 4 things has to happen, because

(continued on next page)

those 4 things include all possibilities. Either you will get what you asked for, you will get something different from what you asked for, you will get what you asked for later than you asked for it, or you will not get anything at all.

Belief in Matthew 18:19-20 and similar verses can be quite dangerous because it can cause people to pray rather than take their medicine or have life-saving surgery. This is particularly dangerous with chronic conditions like heart disease, high blood pressure and diabetes, or with time-critical diseases like cancer. The believer may have faith that they have been cured and no longer need treatment or they may stop taking their medication as a way of proving their faith. Faith can cause people to ignore common-sense health precautions like weight control and proper diet.

Belief in Matthew 18:19-20 can lead to an extremely destructive cycle of guilt. For example, if a child is sick, their Christian parents will pray for their child's health. It sometimes happens that the child's condition worsens no matter how much they pray. If Matthew 18:19-20 is true, the parents now bear full responsibility for their child's sickness, because their child would be healed if they just had enough faith. If their child dies or becomes permanently disabled, they live the rest of their lives with the Bible-based belief that if they had more faith, God would have healed their child. Their grief and sorrow is compounded by overwhelming guilt because of their lack of faith. This is **not** a rare occurrence. I have seen it happen many times.

If Matthew 18:19-20 is true, every Baptist, Presbyterian, Methodist, Catholic or other Christian hospital is a cruel fraud, and every Christian doctor and nurse a fraudster, because they make their patients endure treatments which are often painful and just about always expensive, when they could easily, painlessly and inexpensively cure every single one of their patients if they just had enough faith. If Matthew 18:19-20 is true, a believer could literally walk through a large Surgical Intensive Care Unit and cause every Christian patient to walk out of it in just a few minutes.

Which is the fraud: Matthew 18:19-20 or these health providers? An enormous mass of evidence - medical records, scientific studies, court rulings, state inspections and government licensures - very strongly supports the contention that most of these millions of health professionals are well trained and conscientious, and that their scientifically-based treatments work regardless of the religious beliefs of the caregiver or the patient. Faith supports Matthew 18:19-20.

Penicillin without prayer works better than prayer without penicillin. In a contest between a few pennies' worth of mold extract versus Omnipotent God, the mold extract wins every time. The same could be said for chlorinated drinking water, vaccination, antiseptics, sterile technique, cooking your food enough to kill pathogens or simply washing your hands with strong soap.

1 Holy Spirit → Thousands Of Christian Theological Disputes

In John 16:13-15, Jesus promised, "When he, the Spirit of truth, is come, he will guide you into all truth, for he shall not speak of himself; but whatsoever he shall hear, that shall he speak and he will shew you things to come. He shall glorify me, for he shall receive of mine, and shall shew it unto you. All things that the Father hath are mine, therefore said I, that he shall take of mine, and shall shew it unto you".

Since there is only one Holy Spirit and he is "The Spirit of truth", we should expect him to tell all Christians the same thing, leading to a high degree of agreement on major points of doctrine. This is a common theme in the Bible. See John 14:26, 15:26 and 17:21-23, Romans 12:16 and 15:5-6, 1 Corinthians 1:10-17, 3:3-7 and 11:18-19, Ephesians 4:3-6 and 1 Peter 3:8.

John 16:13-15 is one of the most demonstrably false passages in the Bible. The evidence for this is very clear and provided by Christians themselves. The same evidence also strongly supports the fact that the Bible contradicts itself on major doctrines.

Look in the phone book of any major city which has a large Christian population. You will see listings for dozens if not hundreds of different Christian denominations. There are Catholics, Presbyterians, Baptists, Pentecostals, Seventh Day Adventists, etc. Most of these have further split into smaller, but still completely separate, denominations such as Cumberland Presbyterian, Presbyterian Church USA, Reformed Presbyterian, Reformed Presbyterian Evangelical Synod, Presbyterian Church America, Southern Baptist, Primitive Baptist, Missionary Baptist, American Baptist, Freewill Baptist, Reformed Baptist, National Baptist, Seventh Day Baptist, General Conference Baptist, General Association of Regular Baptist, etc.

If the Holy Spirit is "guiding into all truth" all of these devoted born again Bible believers who are collectively spending billions of hours studying the Bible and sincerely praying that God will help them interpret it correctly, then why do these thousands of denominations disagree on major Bible doctrines so strongly that they have to break off and create their own denomination?

Jesus himself prayed for unity among believers in John 17:11. The Bible condemns such divisiveness in 1 Corinthians 1:10-13 and 3:3-5, so believers are sinning unless they happen to be members of the one only truly correct denomination.

The problem is that the Holy Spirit is not us telling which denomination is the only truly correct one. More precisely, every denomination believes that the Holy Spirit is telling them that their own denomination is the only truly correct one!

Biostatistics vs. Jesus

In Matthew 6:27, Jesus said, "Which of you by taking thought can add one cubit unto his stature?"

Today, hormone treatments are routinely administered to people who suffer from dwarfism to help them grow. These treatments can add a foot or more to a person's height, if they have a hormone deficiency that is stunting their growth.

In addition, it is a well documented fact that improved nutrition and health care has made people living today grow taller than people who lived in earlier historical periods. This has been proven by numerous statistical studies which you can find on the Web. You can easily see this for yourself by going to a museum and looking at suits of armor worn in Ancient, Medieval or Renaissance times. This armor was worn by the big guys of their day, but just about all of it would be too short for today's average male high school senior. Modern improvements in health, nutrition and height happened specifically because millions of scientists have been "taking thought" about these things for over two centuries.

Several modern Bibles translate Matthew 6:27 as longevity, not height. If this is the correct translation, Jesus is even more wrong than he would be if he was referring to height. It is a well documented fact that we are living much longer lives than our ancestors. We are also living much healthier. Diseases such as smallpox, polio, diphtheria, pertussis and plague used to kill millions every year. Now, few people in modern nations know a single person who has ever had one of these diseases. As with height, these improvements have been the direct result of billions of hours of scientific research, because scientists and others were very carefully and thoroughly "taking thought" about how to improve the length and quality of life.

Either way you translate this verse, Jesus was just plain wrong.

Not only does Jesus' statement contradict modern epidemiology and longevity statistics, it contradicts many statements in the Old Testament, which repeatedly claim that following certain lifestyles would lead to a longer, healthier lives. For example, following Kosher diet restrictions is a lot of trouble and requires a lot of "taking thought", but Deuteronomy 7:15 says that if the Hebrews followed Kosher rules, "The Lord will take away from thee all sickness and will put none of the evil diseases of Egypt, which thou knowest, upon thee". (Christians do not follow Old Testament dietary rules. This raises the obvious question of why God would want Christians not to eat food that is as healthy as the food that Jews eat.)

The book of Proverbs provides a lot of guidance about how you could prolong your life. These passages include Proverbs 4:10-11, 4:20-22, 9:10-11 and 10:27, and all require a great deal of "taking thought".

1 Golden Rule, 4 Divine Hypocrisies

In Matthew 7:12, Jesus said, "All things whatsoever ye would that men should do to you, do ye even so to them".

This is often referred to as The Golden Rule, which can also be stated, "Do unto others as you would have others do unto you". Many of the world's major religions have a version of The Golden Rule. Hundreds of years before the New Testament was written, Confucius said, "What you do not want done to yourself, do not do to others", Buddha said, "Hurt not others with that which pains you", and Hindu's holy book, the Baghivad Gita, said, "Good people proceed while considering what is best for others is best for themselves".

Unfortunately, the Golden Rule is one of those rules that Jesus applies to us humans but not to himself. For example:

1 - Imagine you and Jesus traded places: you were Jesus and Jesus was human. Would Jesus want you to make him burn forever in Hell just because he did not believe in you?

2 - Most people would not want to die or be horribly injured in a hurricane, tornado, tsunami, or earthquake. But these "Acts of God" happen every year, killing and wounding many thousands of people. According to Matthew 8:26, Luke 8:25 and 1 Kings 19:11, Jesus has power over natural disasters. But he does not prevent them or prevent thousands of people from being hurt and killed by them. And if they are not Christians when they are killed by natural disasters, they will burn forever in Hell.

3 - Most people would not want to suffer from diseases like cancer, heart disease, stroke or Alzheimer's. But these diseases disable and kill millions every year. Most of us, if we saw someone suffering from a terrible disease or disability which we could easily heal, we would heal them. Matthew 28:18 and Psalm 103:3 say that Jesus has the power to prevent diseases and/or heal them. But he chooses not to do so. In fact, God actually causes many disabilities, according to Exodus 4:11, "Who maketh the dumb, or deaf, or the seeing, or the blind? Have not I the Lord?"

4 - If someone speaks against us or one of our friends, Jesus commands us to forgive them. But if someone speaks against the Holy Spirit, Jesus will never forgive them, according to Matthew 12:31-32, "All manner of sin and blasphemy shall be forgiven unto men: but the blasphemy against the Holy Ghost shall not be forgiven unto men. And whosoever speaketh a word against the Son of man, it shall be forgiven him: but whosoever speaketh against the Holy Ghost, it shall not be forgiven him, neither in this world, neither in the world to come". (This "Unpardonable Sin" is also described in Mark 3:28-30 and Luke 12:10.)

Jesus Commanded Us To Be 490 Times More Forgiving Than God

Matthew 18:21-22 says, "Then came Peter to him [Jesus], and said, Lord, how oft shall my brother sin against me, and I forgive him? Till seven times? Jesus saith unto him, I say not unto thee, until seven times, but until seventy times seven".

When somebody sins against us, no matter how bad it is, we are supposed to forgive them 70 * 7 times. That is probably a metaphor for a much larger number, because some of Jesus' other sayings, such as Matthew 6:14-15, placed no limits on the number of times people are supposed to forgive others.

Jesus created a double standard in this passage because he commanded us to be more forgiving than God is. According to the Bible, we are supposed to forgive the following sins which God does not forgive:

• If someone does not believe what we tell them. But John 3:18 says that if that same person doesn't believe what God tells them, God will make them burn forever in Hell.

• If someone lies to us. But Acts 5:1-10 says that Ananias and Sapphira lied to God and God killed them on the spot.

• If someone speaks against us. But Matthew 12:31-32 says that if someone speaks against the Holy Ghost, God will never forgive them.

• If someone steals our identity. But Mark 3:28-30 and Luke 12:10 says that if someone blasphemes (i.e., impersonates or steals the identity of) the Holy Ghost, God will never forgive them.

• If someone lives on land which God told us is legally ours. Deuteronomy 20:16-17 says, "Of the cities of these people, which the Lord thy God doth give thee for an inheritance, thou shalt save alive nothing that breatheth. But thou shalt utterly destroy them, namely: the Hittites, and the Amorites, the Canaanites, and the Perizzites, the Hivites, and the Jebusites; as the Lord thy God hath commanded thee". See also Deuteronomy 7:1-2.

• If someone misrepresents something we say. Deuteronomy 18:20 says, "The prophet, which shall presume to speak a word in my [God's] name, which I have not commanded him to speak ... even that prophet shall die".

• If a non-Christian invites us to their religious service. Deuteronomy 13:6-10 says this is a death-penalty offense. Galatians 1:8-9 says, "let him be accursed".

• If someone's ancestors made war against our ancestors. 1 Samuel 15:2-3 says, "Thus saith the Lord ... I remember that which Amalek did to Israel, how he laid wait for him in the way, when he came up from Egypt. [This happened over 400 years earlier, see Exodus 17:8-14.] Now go and smite Amalek, and utterly destroy all that they have, and spare them not; but slay both man and woman, infant and suckling."

Believers Works Are Not > Jesus' Works

In John 14:12 Jesus said, "Verily, verily, I say unto you, He that believeth on me, the works that I do shall he do also; and greater works than these shall he do, because I go unto my Father". "Greater than" is a simple mathematical principle. If this passage is true, we should not be able to find anything that Jesus did that is greater than anything his followers can do.

John 14:12 is demonstrably false. Other Bible passages describe at least 4 things that Jesus did, which no Christian can ever come close to accomplishing.

1 - From a Christian point of view, it is difficult to imagine a "greater work" than Jesus dying for the sins of humanity. Jesus claimed to have the power to forgive sins in Matthew 9:2-7, Mark 2:5-11, Luke 5:18-25, 7:48-49 and 24:47, and John 8:24. Jesus also claimed that his blood was, "shed for many for the remission of sins" in Matthew 26:28. Jesus' followers claimed that Jesus, "shall save his people from their sins" in Matthew 1:21 and that he, "taketh away the sin of the world" in John 1:29. If the Bible is true, no other human being can do any of those things because all other humans are sinners.

2 - The one thing that could be "greater" than Jesus dying for people's sins was his Resurrection. According to Christian theology, Jesus' Resurrection was different from, and much better than, other "raisings from the dead" performed by Jesus' Apostles (e.g., Acts 20:9-12), because those people whom the Apostles raised eventually physically died again, but Jesus did not die again. No other human has ever resurrected himself from the dead, or will ever be able to.

3 - According to the Bible, Jesus has abolished death. 2 Timothy 1:10 says, "Our Saviour Jesus Christ, who hath abolished death, and hath brought life and immortality to light through the gospel". This has a triple meaning to many conservative Christians because they believe that the Bible claims there are three kinds of death. The first kind of death is spiritual death, described in Genesis chapters 2-3. The second kind of death is physical death, which is the normal kind of death that occurs when essential life functions such as brain activity cease in a person's body. We are still waiting for Jesus to abolish physical death, but he assures us in Revelation chapters 20-22 that eventually he will do so. The third kind of death, also called the "second death" in Revelation 20:14, is everlasting punishment for people that God disapproves of. Although sinners will endure eternal damnation, it is "abolished" in the sense that Jesus' followers will be saved from it. Not one of Jesus' followers has ever "abolished" any form of death, or will ever be able to do so.

4 - Jesus was God, according to John 1:1, John 10:30 and many other verses. If so, Jesus created the Universe. No Christian has ever topped that either.

Another "Greater Than" Goof

In John 14:28, Jesus said, "My Father is greater than I.". This is one of several Bible verses where Jesus himself clearly said that he and his father were separate and unequal, and that he was the lesser of the two.

• In Matthew 24:36-37, Jesus said that God had knowledge that he did not have, "But of that day and hour knoweth no man, no, not the angels of heaven, but my Father only. But as the days of Noe [Noah] were, so shall also the coming of the Son of man be". Mark 13:32 says something very similar.

• In John 12:47-49, Jesus said that he took orders from his father, "The Father which sent me, he gave me a commandment, what I should say, and what I should speak". Bible never says that Jesus commanded God.

• John 5:26-27 says, "For as the Father hath life in Himself, so hath he given to the Son to have life in himself, and hath given him authority to execute judgment also, because he is the Son of Man". Matthew 28:18 also says that God gave authority to Jesus. The Bible never says that Jesus gave authority to God.

Other verses are equally dogmatic in claiming that Jesus was equal with God:

• In John 10:30, Jesus said, " I and my Father are one".

• John 14:9 says, "Jesus saith unto him, Have I been so long time with you, and yet hast thou not known me, Philip? He that hath seen me hath seen the Father; and how sayest thou then, Shew us the Father?"

• Colossians 2:9 says, "For in him [Christ] dwelleth all the fullness of the Godhead bodily".

• 1 John 5:7 says, "There are three that bear record in heaven, the Father, the Word [Jesus, see John 1:1-3], and the Holy Ghost: and these three are one".

Just about all modern Christians believe that Jesus is completely equal to and unified with God the Father. In the early days of Christianity, however, Christians violently disagreed with each other about this essential doctrine.

This is known as the "Arian Controversy" because Arius was the leader of Christians who believed that Jesus was not coequal with God the Father. Although the Roman Emperor Constantine[2] referred to this controversy as "silly actions worthy of inexperienced children, and not of priests or reasonable men", he convened the Council of Nicea to try to get Christians to agree with each other. His attempts were unsuccessful and the Christian church remained split on this issue for over 50 years until Emperor Theodosius decreed that all Arian church leaders were to be exiled, fined ten pounds of gold per person and have all of their property confiscated by the government[3]. Jesus was made coequal with God at the point of a Roman sword, not by divine revelation or Biblical debate.

Jesus' Dietary Dilemma #1

In Mark 7:15-19, Jesus said, "There is nothing from without a man, that entering into him can defile him ... whatsoever thing from without entereth into the man, it cannot defile him, because it entereth not into his heart, but into the belly, and goeth out into the draught, purging all meats?". In Matthew 15:11-17, Jesus said, "Not that which goeth into the mouth defileth a man, but that which cometh out of the mouth, this defileth a man ... Do not ye yet understand, that whatsoever entereth in at the mouth goeth into the belly, and is cast out into the draught?"

"Nothing" is a precise mathematical term. If you ask your bank how much money you owe them and they reply "nothing", you know exactly what that means.

In plain English, Jesus said that there is "nothing" that you can eat or drink which will cause you to sin or "defile yourself", because everything you eat or drink simply passes through your digestive tract and is excreted.

But other Bible verses make it clear that there is at least one thing "that entering into him can defile" a person: large amounts of alcoholic beverages. Jesus' followers are commanded to "be not drunk with wine" in Ephesians 5:18 and to avoid "excess of wine" in 1 Peter 4:3. Older church members must be, "sober ... temperate ... and not given to much wine" according to Titus 2:2-3. Church leaders are required to be, "not given to wine ... sober" by Titus 1:7-8, "not given to wine" by 1 Timothy 3:3 and "not given to much wine" by 1 Timothy 3:8.

These passages were literally interpreted by Christian conservatives in the 1800's and early 1900's, and were the basis for the Temperance Movement, which opposed all forms of alcoholic beverages and had an enormous political impact. This movement peaked in 1919 with the passage of the 18th amendment to the US Constitution, which prohibited "intoxicating liquors" and was repealed in 1933.

Today, many Christian denominations do permit the consumption of moderate amounts of alcohol, though all are united in their opposition to excessive drinking. This opposition is consistent with the above verses from Ephesians, Peter, Titus and Timothy, and equally inconsistent with the statements of Jesus quoted above.

The Bible's prohibitions against excessive alcohol consumption are almost universally believed by modern Christians to include all forms of substance abuse. Although this is consistent with the spirit of the Bible's prohibitions against excessive alcohol consumption (as well as being one of those rare Biblical concepts that I wholeheartedly support), it merely adds to the list of things that contradict the statements by Jesus in Mark 7:15-19 and Matthew 15:11-17. Certainly, few if any Christians would deny that it is a very serious sin - that it would certainly "defile" you - to eat or drink even a very small amount of LSD, heroin, crack cocaine, crystal meth or many other illegal mood altering substances.

Jesus' Dietary Dilemma #2

In Mark 16:17-18, Jesus said, "And these signs shall follow them that believe. ... If they drink any deadly thing, it shall not harm them".

"Any" is a precise mathematical term. If you go to a buffet restaurant and they tell you that you can eat "any" food on the buffet, you know exactly what that means.

Jesus promised that if believers drink (but not necessarily eat) "any deadly thing" they will not die; they will not even be harmed.

Christians will argue that there are two exceptions to this. The first exception is that you should not drink excessive amounts of alcohol. (See Jesus' Dietary Dilemma #1, above.) The second is that you should not knowingly drink anything harmful because that is "testing" God, which Jesus prohibited in Matthew 4:7. We can let them have those exceptions because there are more serious, easily quantifiable problems with Mark 16:17-18.

Millions of people, including Christians, legitimately drink "deadly things" every day when they take liquid medications. Modern medications can have enormous benefits when used properly, but accidental overdoses kill thousands of people every year. No drug has any different dosage or labeling based on whether or not the patient is a Christian. This has substantial clinical implications because in some treatments, such as some types of cancer chemotherapy or some treatments for serious infections, the most effective dose is the maximum amount that the patient can endure without dangerous side effects. It is simply absurd to suggest that Christians respond to liquid medications any differently from anyone else.

Another common "deadly thing" that people drink every day is polluted water. Many people who live in economically or technologically disadvantaged areas don't have any choice - they must either drink the bad water or die of thirst. If it was really true that "if they drink any deadly thing, it shall not harm them", you could go to some of the most unsanitary regions of the world and dramatically reduce the rates of cholera, diphtheria and childhood diarrhea by simply getting people to believe in Jesus. This is absurd. When you are drinking water that is contaminated with pathogens - chlorine, microfiltering or boiling beats Jesus every time.

Chemical pollutants are also a substantial risk for drinking water. Once again, Jesus is wrong. Central Alabama in the United States is one of the most conservatively Christian areas of the world. In the early 2000's, several court cases[4] determined that tens of thousands of people, a very large percentage of whom were Christians, were sickened and many died from drinking water that they did not know was contaminated by dioxin and other chemical wastes. No one dared to argue that the corporate polluters could not be held liable because Christians were unaffected by polluted water.

Jesus vs. Hundreds of Thousands of Copying Errors

In Matthew 5:18, Jesus said, "Verily I say unto you, till heaven and earth pass, one jot or one tittle shall in no wise pass from the law, till all be fulfilled". "The Law" in this verse is Hebrew Law contained in the Old Testament, i.e., the first 5 books of the Bible, also called the Law of Moses or the Pentateuch.

These words of Jesus prophesy that not "one jot or one tittle" shall pass from God's Law until the earth ceases to exist. "Jot" and "tittle" are portions of individual Hebrew characters similar to crossing a "T" or dotting an "i" in English. Jesus was emphatically saying that every detail, every word and every letter of God's Law will be here as long as the earth is.

The earth is still here, but modern scholarship knows of hundreds of ancient and medieval Hebrew manuscripts which differ from each other in thousands of ways. There is even a whole discipline of Biblical scholarship, "Textual Analysis", devoted to trying to figure out what the "original" manuscripts looked like based on manuscripts which are separated from the "original" manuscripts by hundreds of years, and for some passages, over 1,000 years. Although these scholars do agree on some passages, they do not agree on every "jot and tittle" of all of them.

The number of variations between manuscripts is so large that no one has an exact number. Most Bible scholars estimate the number of variations to be many thousands for the Law of Moses; there are hundreds of thousands of variations if all books of the Old Testament are considered. The discovery of the Dead Sea Scrolls, which themselves date from at least 300 years to more than 1,300 years after the writing of the "original" manuscripts, only complicated the issue by adding thousands more variations. So even if a manuscript exists which is identical to the "original" manuscripts, we do not know which one it is, and therefore the knowledge of every "jot and tittle" of the Law of Moses has been lost to modern Bible believers.

This is very much in contrast to some other bodies of ancient law. For example, Hammurabi ruled Babylon no later than 1700 BCE, hundreds of years before Bible scholars believe that Moses lived. You can see over 3800 lines of text, containing 282 of Hammurabi's laws, on a 7-foot high stone stela (column) on display at the Louvre in Paris, France. This stela is topped by a bas-relief carving showing Hammurabi receiving these laws directly from the god Shemesh, and is believed to date from the lifetime of Hammurabi himself.

Although I have discussed only Old Testament Law on this page, this discussion would apply equally well to the entire Christian Bible. There are literally hundreds of thousands of variations between manuscripts. Many of these disputed passages involve essential doctrines such as the Resurrection (Mark 16:9-20) and the Trinity (1 John 5:7-8)

Jesus Was Short By At Least 4 Prophets

In Luke 4:24, Jesus said, "And he said, Verily I say unto you, No prophet is accepted in his own country". John 4:44 says, "Jesus himself testified that a prophet hath no honor in his own country". Matthew 13:57 says, "Jesus said unto them, 'A prophet is not without honor, save in his own country and in his own house'". Mark 6:4 says, "Jesus said unto them, 'A prophet is not without honor, but in his own country'".

If these statements by Jesus were correct, we should not be able to find a prophet that was accepted or honored in his/her own country. But at least four Old Testament prophets were accepted and honored in their own country.

Deborah was a prophetess that judged the nation of Israel, according to Judges 4:4. Judges 4:24 says, "The children of Israel prospered" while she was judge.

The prophet Samuel lived in the land of the tribe of Ephraim, according to 1 Samuel 1:1-28. 1 Samuel 3:20 says, "All Israel from Dan [the very northern boundary of Israel] even to Beer-sheba [at the very southern boundary of Israel] knew that Samuel was established to be a prophet of the Lord".

The Bible certainly claims that David was accepted and honored in his own country - he was king. It also claims that he was certainly a prophet, because it says that David also wrote many Psalms, the including some that supposedly contained prophecies about Jesus:

- Psalm 110, which Hebrews 5:5-6 says is a fulfilled prophecy
- Psalm 8, which Matthew 21:15-16 says is a fulfilled prophecy
- Psalm 41, which John 13:18 says is a fulfilled prophecy
- Psalm 35:19, which John 15:24-25 says is a fulfilled prophecy

Although each of these "prophecies" is demonstrably bogus (many are refuted in my book "100 False Bible Prophecies"), Christians believe they are prophecies made by David, thereby establishing him as a prophet who was honored in his own country, invalidating Jesus' statements in Luke 4:24, John 4:44, Matthew 13:57 and Mark 6:4.

King Solomon was also a prophet. An Old Testament prophet could prophesy in two ways. The first was to predict the future. The second was to teach about God. Although the Bible contains no predictions by Solomon, it claims that Solomon wrote three books of the Bible: Proverbs, Ecclesiastes and Song of Solomon. This certainly qualifies Solomon as a "prophet". Being king would certainly constitute acceptance and honor. Also, God said he would give "honor" to Solomon in 1 Kings 3:13. So Jesus was wrong again.

Chapter 2

Math Mistakes About Jesus

Jesus' followers included people who should have been quite good with numbers. These include Matthew, a tax collector, Luke, a physician, and Paul, who claimed to have been educated by Gamaliel, the famous Pharisee.

Unfortunately, Jesus' followers shared his difficulty with numbers. Not only did they frequently fail to get their figures right, they often contradicted each other.

Although these numerical errors cause great difficulties for people who believe that the Bible was written by God, for others they are the source of profound insights about the Bible itself and the people who wrote it.

Some of the Bible's numerical errors surrounding Jesus enable us to trace the evolution of "The Jesus Myth" among his followers. The numbers clearly changed as time passed. Events which would have been impossible to ignore and would have had enormous evidential value if they had really occurred were mysteriously omitted from later reports of the same people, places and time periods.

Although every numerical contradiction in the Bible casts doubt on its "infallibility", some of the numerical contradictions surrounding Jesus reveal something far more damaging to the belief that the Bible is without error: the writers of some of the books of the Bible very obviously believed that other books of the Bible were not infallible.

Most troubling of all, however, is that examination of the numerical errors and mathematical contradictions penned by Jesus' followers indicates that they sometimes deliberately suppressed, misused or falsified Biblical evidence that contradicted what they wrote about Jesus. Other math errors lead us to the conclusion that the writers of the New Testament distorted the clear meaning of Old Testament passages as they attempted to prove things that the original texts could not possibly have intended and that no objective reader could possibly have understood these passages to mean. This is not what you would expect from a book that claims to be humanity's ultimate written source of absolute truth.

The theological significance of these errors and contradictions cannot be overstated, because they provide convincing evidence that the writers of the New Testament were wrong about essential facts about Jesus, such as his ancestry, fulfilment of prophecies, perfection and divinity, as well as major events in his life such as his crucifixion and resurrection.

Matthew's "Prophecy" Is Wrong By Over 700 Years

Isaiah 7:14 says, "Therefore the Lord himself shall give you a sign. Behold, a virgin shall conceive, and bear a son, and shall call his name Immanuel". This is quoted in Matthew 1:23, and is one of the most famous "prophecies" allegedly about Jesus.

To find definitive proofs that Matthew 1:23 is wrong, we need look no farther than the two verses immediately after Isaiah 7:14, which clearly show that this passage cannot possibly be talking about Jesus Christ. Isaiah 7:15-16 says, "Butter and honey shall he eat, that he may know to refuse the evil, and choose the good. For before the child shall know to refuse the evil, and choose the good, the land that thou abhorrest shall be forsaken of both her kings". The New American Standard Bible uses modern English, "The land whose two kings you dread will be forsaken [Revised Standard Bible says 'deserted']". Moffatt translates this as, "The land whose two kings are your terror shall be desolate".

The first proof that Isaiah 7:14-16 cannot be talking about Jesus is that there was never a time "before" Jesus knew "to refuse the evil and choose the good". According to Colossians 2:9 and John 10:30, Jesus is God. According to Hebrews 13:8, Jesus does not change.

Secondly, Isaiah 7:14-16 gives a definite time period for Immanuel's infancy and childhood. This "prophecy" says that two kings will be removed from power and/or their lands will be deserted before Immanuel is old enough to choose evil or good. These kings are repeatedly named in Isaiah chapter 7 - Syria's king Rezin in Isaiah 7:8 and Israel/Samaria/Ephraim's king Pekah son of Remaliah in Isaiah 7:9. Both are named in Isaiah 7:1.

2 Kings 16:9 says that Rezin was killed around 740 BCE. 2 Kings 15:30 says that Pekah was killed about the same time. 2 Kings 16:9 also says that the king of Assyria deported all of the Syrians from Damascus to Kir, an Assyrian district between the Caspian and Black seas. About 9 years later, 2 Kings 17:6 says that the king of Assyria deported all of Israel (i.e., all of the Hebrew tribes except Judah, Benjamin and Levi) to various Assyrian cities. All of these events happened over 700 years before Jesus is believed to have been born.

It should also be pointed out that the Hebrew word translated "virgin" in Isaiah 7:14 is "almah", which does not necessarily mean "woman who has never had sex". "Almah" is translated "maid" in Exodus 2:8 and Proverbs 30:19, and "damsel" in Psalm 68:25. The Hebrew word that always means "virgin" is "bethulah", which is not used in Isaiah 7:14. Although ancient gods impregnated human virgins enthusiastically and frequently (e.g., Romulus, Remus, Dionysus, Hercules), the Hebrew text provides no reason to believe that Isaiah 7:14 predicted a virgin birth.

Matthew's Dirty Little Secret About Jesus' Ancestors

One of the Bible's most widely believed prophecies about the Messiah/Christ is that he had to be descended from King David, as stated in Jeremiah 23:5, "Behold, the days come, saith the Lord, that I will raise unto David a righteous branch, and a king shall reign and prosper, and shall execute judgement and justice in the earth".

This belief is so important that the gospels of Matthew and Luke both list genealogies for Jesus. Those genealogies irreconcilably contradict each other, but that is not a math error and so it is out of the scope of this book. Matthew's genealogy, however, contains a math error which leads to a startling discovery about Jesus.

1 Chronicles 3:10-16 lists the generations from David's son Solomon to the Babylonian captivity. Matthew 1:6-11 gives the same list, but omits 4 names:

Generation	1 Chronicles 3:10-16	Matthew 1:6-11
1	Solomon	Solomon
2	Rehoboam	Rehoboam
3	Abia	Abijah
4	Asa	Asa
5	Jehoshaphat	Jehoshaphat
6	Joram	Jehoram
7	Ahaziah	Uzziah
8	Joash	*Missing*
9	Amaziah	*Missing*
10	Azariah	*Missing*
11	Jotham	Jotham
12	Ahaz	Ahaz
13	Hezekiah	Hezekiah
14	Manasseh	Manasseh
15	Amon	Amon
16	Josiah	Josiah
17	Jehoiakim	*Missing*
18	Jeconiah	Jeconiah

If the writer of Matthew had only listed the generations and not counted them for us, these omissions would not necessarily be an error because Biblical genealogies do sometimes skip generations. But Matthew 1:17 says, "**All** the generations ... from David until the carrying away into Babylon are **fourteen** generations". 1 Chronicles 3:10-16, as well as the details provided in the books of Samuel, Kings and Chronicles, describe the reigns of Hebrew kings for **eighteen** generations from Solomon to Jeconiah.

(continued on the next page)

So the Gospel of Matthew is incorrect if the "historical" book of 1 Chronicles is telling the truth. This appears to be trivial until you closely examine one of the kings whom the author of Matthew omitted. Although it is unclear why he omitted Joash, Amaziah and Azariah, his reason for omitting Jehoiakim is clear and constitutes damning evidence against the truthfulness of the Gospel of Matthew.

If Jehoiakim was an ancestor of Jesus, then the Bible says that Jesus could not be the Christ! Jeremiah 36:30 says, "Thus saith the Lord of Jehoiakim king of Judah; He shall have none to sit upon the throne of David". This is more clear in some modern translations. For example, the Moffatt translation says, "No descendant of his shall ever sit upon the throne of David".

First century Jews believed that the Bible prophesied that the Messiah would be King of the Jews. Matthew 2:1-6 says,

"Now when Jesus was born in Bethlehem of Judaea in the days of Herod the king, behold, there came wise men from the east to Jerusalem, saying, Where is he that is born King of the Jews? For we have seen his star in the east, and are come to worship him. When Herod the king had heard these things, he was troubled and all Jerusalem with him. And when he had gathered all the chief priests and scribes of the people together, he demanded of them where Christ should be born. And they said unto him, In Bethlehem of Judaea: for thus it is written by the prophet, And thou Bethlehem, in the land of Juda, art not the least among the princes of Juda, for out of thee shall come a Governor, that shall rule my people Israel."

Jesus himself claimed to be King of the Jews in Matthew 27:11, Mark 15:2, Luke 23:3 and John 1:49-51. His Apostles repeated his claim in Matthew 21:4-5 and John 12:13-15.

This kingship had a very specific name: the Throne of David. This is based on Isaiah 9:6-7, "For unto us a child is born, unto us a son is given, and the government shall be upon his shoulder: and his name shall be called Wonderful, Counsellor, the mighty God, the everlasting Father, the Prince of Peace. Of the increase of his government and peace there shall be no end, upon the throne of David". According to Luke 1:32, an angel announced that Jesus fulfilled this prophecy, "He [Jesus] shall be great, and shall be called the Son of the Highest: and the Lord God shall give unto him the throne of his father David".

But if Jeremiah was correct, no ruler of Israel, sitting on the Throne of David, could have Jehoiakim as an ancestor. Jesus was excluded by Jeremiah 36:30, which claims to be a prophecy from God himself. If Matthew correctly reports that Josiah and Jechoniah (and therefore Jehoiakim) are Jesus' ancestors, Jesus cannot be Christ.

Dating The First Christmas ("Christ-Mass") Is A Mess

The birth of Jesus Christ, if it really occurred, was arguably the most important event in human history. Certainly its importance to Christians cannot be overstated. If Jesus Christ was never born, Christianity disintegrates into an ash heap of discredited mythology. But this indispensable event is replete with historical errors and contradictions.

Christians themselves cannot agree on the date of Jesus' birth. Protestant and Catholic Christians celebrate Christmas on December 25, but many Eastern Christians in Russia, Egypt, Armenia, Ukraine and Serbia use the Julian calendar, which means that they celebrate Christmas in January, almost two weeks later than western Christians. Many Bible scholars believe that neither date is accurate, because December and January are quite cold in Bethlehem and Luke 2:8 says that there were "shepherds abiding in the field, keeping watch over their flock by night". I was actually in Bethlehem on Christmas Eve in 1972; the temperature was below freezing that night and all of the shepherds were inside trying to stay warm. Saint Clement of Alexandria[1], writing around 200 CE, reported that some Christians believed that Jesus was born on April 19 and others believed the day was actually May 20. Clement himself claimed that November 17 was the correct date.

December 25 was a holiday long before Jesus because of its proximity to the winter Solstice, which occurs on December 21. Before the invention of telescopes, it was difficult to see that the sun was rising higher in the sky until several days after the Solstice, therefore December 25 was often used. There was a population explosion of pagan divine nativities on December 25: it was believed to be the birth date of Dionysus, Mithras, Horus and others. December 25 was the date of the "Yule", i.e., the feast of the god Frey[2] in pagan northern Europe. It was also the date of numerous Roman festivals, such as the festival of Sol Invictus, the Saturnalia and the Brumalia, as well as the Greek festival of Dionysus. Christmas is a recycled pagan holiday.

Jesus' birth day is not the only problem. His birth year fares even worse when historically examined.

Matthew 2:1 very clearly says, "Jesus was born in Bethlehem of Judaea in the days of Herod the king", and then describes Herod's attempt to murder the young Jesus. According to Matthew 2:16, Jesus could have been up to two years old when Herod tried to kill him. The problem is that Herod died in 4 BCE, an historical fact which is widely accepted among historians and Bible scholars. Even bastions of conservatism such as the Scofield Reference Bible admit to the theologically disturbing fact that Jesus would have to have been born at least 4 years "Before Christ".

(continued on next page)

Luke 2:2 says that the birth of Jesus could have occurred no earlier than "when Cyrenius was governor of Syria". Cyrenius, sometimes translated as Quirinius or Kyrenios, did not become governor of Syria until 6 CE[3]. So Luke and Matthew contradict each other by at least ten years when reporting the birth date of their Savior.

Christian apologists have to fabricate some history to try to argue against this contradiction. They theorize that Cyrenius was actually governor of Syria twice - once during the reign of Herod and a second time around 6 CE. This speculation is unsupported by any historical evidence. Despite abundant historical records from this era, not one contemporary or near-contemporary historian reports that Cyrenius was governor of Syria while Herod was alive. Josephus, the first century Jewish historian, made no mention of Cyrenius during his extensive discussion of the Middle East during the time of Herod, a discussion which fills 43 chapters of his books. But Josephus did mention Cyrenius twice in relation to the final days of the reign of Archelaus, a son of Herod who reigned after his father's death (see Matthew 2:22). Caesar removed Archelaus from power in 6 CE[4]. Josephus' Antiquities 17:13:5, says that Cyrenius "was sent by Caesar to ... sell the house of Archelaus". Antiquities 18:1:1, says, "Cyrenius came himself into Judea, which was now added to the province of Syria ... to dispose of Archelaus' money".

Josephus repeatedly stated that Quintillus Varus was the governor of Syria during the last years of the reign of Herod. Antiquities, 17.5.2 says, "Now Quintillus Varus was at this time at Jerusalem, being sent to succeed Saturninus as governor of Syria, and was come as a counselor to Herod, who had desired his advice in his present affairs". See also Antiquities 17.5.3 thru 17.5.7, 17.9.3, and 17.10.1 thru 17.10.10.

Some apologists claim that the translators of the King James Bible made a mistake when they translated Luke 2:2. The King James says, "This taxing was first made when Cyrenius was governor of Syria". They assert that the original Greek really means something like, "This taxing was made the first time that Cyrenius was governor of Syria", or maybe, "This was the first taxing, before Cyrenius was governor of Syria". The Greek text itself clearly does not support these interpretations. You do not have to be a Greek scholar to see this, because many experts in the Biblical Greek language have already done it for us. The translations of Luke 2:2 in the New American Standard, Revised Standard, New King James, Rheims, Today's English and New International Bible are all very similar to the King James translation. This widespread agreement between well-respected translations indicates that there is widespread consensus among Bible scholars, linguists and textual analysts that this passage means something very close to what the King James Bible says it means, i.e., that the Gospel of Luke very clearly claims that Jesus was born while Cyrenius was governor of Syria, and does not imply that Cyrenius was governor more than once.

Prophecy: Out Of Context, 570 Years Late, Proving God Is Immoral

Jeremiah 31:15 says, "Thus saith the Lord: A voice was heard in Ramah, lamentation, and bitter weeping, Rachel weeping for her children refused to be comforted for her children, because they were not".

Matthew 2:16-18 claims that Jeremiah 31:15 is supposedly a prophecy that was fulfilled when Herod murdered of all of the male infants and toddlers in Bethlehem. This "prophecy" is as completely wrong as a prediction can be.

• Bethlehem was not Ramah. Bethlehem is located 5 miles south of Jerusalem, in the land of the tribe of Judah. The Old Testament lists three cities named "Ramah": Joshua 18:21-25 describes one in the land of the tribe of Benjamin, Joshua 19:32-26 describes another in the land of the tribe of Naphtali, and 1 Samuel 1:1 and 7:15-17 describe yet another one in the land of the tribe of Ephraim. All of these were located several hours or even several days journeys north of Jerusalem. Three verses in Jeremiah chapter 31 - verses 6, 9, 18 and 20 - specifically refer to "Ephraim". The town of "Rama" in Ephraim was located about a day's journey north of Bethlehem.

• Bethlehem was the "City of David" according to Luke 2:4. David was descended from Leah, not Rachel, according to Matthew 1:2-6, Luke 3:31-33 and Genesis 29:32-30:1. David's descendants were not mentioned in this "prophecy".

• Matthew reports that the children were murdered, but the two verses immediately following Jeremiah 31:15 say that the children would return to their mothers. "Thus saith the Lord; Refrain thy voice from weeping and thine eyes from tears, for thy work shall be rewarded, saith the Lord, and they shall come again from the land of the enemy. And there is hope in thine end, saith the Lord, that thy children shall come again to their own border" (Jeremiah 31:16-17).

• Since the children would return to their mothers, the "prophecy" in Jeremiah 31:15 would have to be fulfilled while at least some of those mothers were still alive. But Biblical literalists believe that the book of Jeremiah was written around 610-580 BCE, and the events in Matthew chapter 2 are believed to have occurred around 6-4 BCE, a difference of over 570 years.

So this "prophecy" was wrong about:

Prediction	Jeremiah	Matthew
Where the crime would happen	Ramah	Bethlehem
When the crime would happen:	610-580 BCE	6-4 BCE
Who the victims would be	Descendants Of Rachel	Of Leah
What the crime was	Kidnapping	Murder

It was **not** correct about a single prediction.

(continued on next page)

Another evidence that Jeremiah's prophecy was not referring to children in Bethlehem around 6-4 BCE (or that this passage in Matthew is a complete myth) is the fact that not one person in Bethlehem used this prophecy to save the life of a single boy. If you were a parent and heard the slightest hint that someone was going to harm your child, you would do everything you could to protect them. People in Bethlehem were Jewish; they knew their Bibles. They were within a short walk of Jerusalem, the location of the world's greatest Old Testament scholars. But God had to warn Joseph and the wise men in dreams, and no other human knew about the impending slaughter.

All of the above pales, however, in comparison to the moral implications of this "prophecy" if Matthew is right. Suppose a person knew beforehand that someone was going to murder some children and had the power to stop them, but didn't. Then he actually watched as these murders were committed (Proverbs 15:3) and made a point of telling you that he knew all about this in advance and did not stop it.

Would you admire this person as a great moral leader? No. You would tell the police and the courts would send him to prison. This is not speculation, it is the law. For example, on April 19, 1995, Timothy McVeigh detonated over two tons of explosives a few feet from a day care center full of children in the Murrah Federal building in Oklahoma City. 15 children and 153 adults were killed. Michael Fourtier knew about McVeigh's plans in advance and could have easily prevented these murders by telling the police, but he did not say anything to the police until after the crime was committed. Because of this, Fourtier was sentenced to many years in prison.

If a person knows in advance that a murder will be committed and does nothing to stop it, United States criminal law says that person committed a felony. If God knows in advance that a mass murder will be committed and does nothing to stop it, Bible believers say that God performed a miracle.

Christians argue that this slaughter was necessary because God prophesied it and if it hadn't come true then God would have been proven wrong. But every human I know would gladly admit to making a mistake if it would save lives. Besides, all-knowing God could have simply not predicted it would happen.

As bad as this is, however, it pales in comparison to God's own mass murders of children. In Numbers 31:17, God commanded, "Now therefore kill every male among the little ones", resulting in the murders of tens of thousands of boys. In 1 Samuel 15:3, God commanded, "Utterly destroy all that they have and spare them not, but slay both man and woman, infant and suckling". In Deuteronomy 20:16-17, God commanded, "Save alive nothing that breatheth, but thou shalt utterly destroy them, namely, the Hittites, and the Amorites, and the Canaanites, and the Perizzites, the Hivites and the Jebusites", resulting in the murders of over 3,000,000 people (see "God Ordered > 3,000,000 Violations Of Thou Shalt Not Murder" in Chapter 3).

Zero, Three or "All" Temptations for Jesus?

James 1:13 says, "God cannot be tempted with evil". Since Christians believe that Jesus is God, as stated in Colossians 2:9 and John 10:30, we would expect the Bible to report zero temptations for Jesus. Not so.

Matthew, Mark and Luke report that Jesus was tempted by Satan while he was in the wilderness for 40 days. They report 3 temptations: turn stones into bread, test God by throwing himself off of the roof of the Temple, and bow down to Satan.

Not to be outdone, Hebrews 4:15 says, "We have not an high priest which cannot be touched with the feeling of our infirmities, but was in **all** points tempted like as we are, yet without sin". Hebrews 2:18 and 1 Corinthians 10:13 claim that these temptations enable Jesus to help Christians resist temptation, because he has endured the same temptations himself.

If Jesus really is God, then Hebrews 4:15 is untrue because there are many human temptations that Jesus could not possibly have experienced. Jesus could not be tempted to be an atheist because he was God. Also, the belief that Jesus, "was in all points tempted", requires some very sordid beliefs about this supposedly "perfect" man, because it means that he felt a real desire to commit sins so repulsive that even being tempted indicates the presence of serious psychopathology, such as bestiality and pedophilia.

Some temptations require the prior commissions of other sins to be experienced. One example is the intense craving (temptation to abuse a drug) that an addict feels when suffering from convulsions or delirium while going through withdrawal, because you must commit the sin of addiction before experiencing withdrawal.

There are several more types of sins which Jesus could not possibly have been tempted to commit. Jesus could not be tempted like Abraham was when God ordered Abraham to kill his son Isaac in Genesis 22:1-13. If Jesus killed anyone, he could take them up to be with him in Heaven so he would not be away from them for a minute, or he could simply raise them from the dead.

Several Biblical characters lied to save someone else's life. For examples, see Exodus 1:15-20, Joshua 2:3-6, 1 Samuel 19:11-18 and 2 Samuel 17:17-22. Jesus could not be tempted to lie to save someone else's life because Jesus was omnipotent, so he had many non-deceitful ways of saving someone's life which were unavailable to the Biblical liars referenced above (e.g., Luke 4:28-30). Or he could just let the person be killed and then raise them from the dead (e.g., John 11:1-44).

Jesus created an Inescapable Sin in Matthew 5:32, "Whosoever shall put away his wife, saving for the cause of fornication, causeth her to commit adultery". Jesus could not be tempted to commit this sin because it only applied to married women. For more information, please see "Inescapable Adulteries > Zero" in Chapter 4.

30 or 17 Pieces Of Silver And The Wrong Prophet

Matthew 27:9-10 misquotes the Old Testament and attributes the quote to the wrong prophet. The author of Matthew says that the quote came from Jeremiah, but really it is found in Zechariah. Differences are *italicized*.

Matthew 27:9-10 says, "Then was fulfilled that which was spoken by Jeremy [Jeremiah] the prophet, saying, *And* they *took* the thirty pieces of silver, *the price of him that was valued, whom they of the children of Israel did value, And gave them for the* potter's *field, as the Lord appointed me*".

Zechariah 11:12-13 says, "And I said unto them, If ye think good, give me my price; and if not, forbear. *So* they *weighed for my price* thirty pieces of silver. *And the Lord said unto me, Cast it unto the* potter: *a goodly price that I was priced at of them. And I took* the thirty pieces of silver, *and cast them to the* potter *in the house of the Lord*".

Some apologists[5] claim that Matthew was actually referring to Jeremiah chapter 32, which is so different from Matthew 27:9-10 that any comparison is meaningless. Jeremiah 32:8-10 says, "So Hanameel mine uncle's son came to me in the court of the prison according to the word of the Lord, and said unto me, Buy my field, I pray thee, that is in Anathoth, which is in the country of Benjamin: for the right of inheritance is thine, and the redemption is thine; buy it for thyself. Then I knew that this was the word of the Lord. And I bought the field of Hanameel my uncle's son, that was in Anathoth, and weighed him the money, even **seventeen** shekels of silver. And I subscribed the evidence, and sealed it, and took witnesses, and weighed him the money in the balances".

Conservative Bible scholar John Haley is more honest, "Here is obviously a mistake"[6].

It should be pointed out that neither Zechariah 11:12-13 nor Jeremiah 32:8-10 actually predict anything. Both of them very clearly speak in the past tense about things that had already happened by the time these passages were written. Also, neither of them mention the Messiah/Christ. Whichever passage(s) that the author of Matthew used was twisted into an interpretation that no one before Matthew could have imagined it meant.

Jewish scholar Aryeh Kaplan sums it up well, "Early Christians ... went over the entire [Jewish] Bible with a fine tooth comb, looking for any evidence, however flimsy, to prove that Jesus was the Messiah and that their entire logical structure was in accord with ancient Jewish teachings. In many cases, they were not above using verses out of context, changing texts, and even mistranslating them, in order to prove their point."[7]

One Or Two Blind Men?

Matthew 20:29-34 tells the story of Jesus healing two blind men.

"And as they departed from Jericho, a great multitude followed him. And, behold, **two blind men** sitting by the way side, when **they** heard that Jesus passed by, cried out, saying, Have mercy on **us**, O Lord, thou son of David. And the multitude rebuked **them**, because **they** should hold their peace: but **they** cried the more, saying, Have mercy on **us**, O Lord, thou son of David. And Jesus stood still, and called **them**, and said, What will ye that I shall do unto you? **They** say unto him, Lord, that **our** eyes may be opened. So Jesus had compassion on **them**, and touched **their** eyes, and immediately **their** eyes received sight, and **they** followed him".

But Mark 10:46-52 tells the same story differently.

"As he went out of Jericho with his disciples and a great number of people, **blind Bartimaeus**, the son of Timaeus, sat by the highway side begging. And when **he** heard that it was Jesus of Nazareth, **he** began to cry out, and say, Jesus, thou son of David, have mercy on **me**. And many charged **him** that **he** should hold **his** peace, but **he** cried the more a great deal, Thou son of David, have mercy on **me**. And Jesus stood still, and commanded **him** to be called. And they call the blind man, saying unto **him**, Be of good comfort, rise; he calleth thee. And **he**, casting away **his** garment, rose, and came to Jesus. And Jesus answered and said unto **him**, What wilt thou that I should do unto thee? The blind **man** said unto him, Lord, that I might receive my sight. And Jesus said unto **him**, Go thy way; thy faith hath made thee whole. And immediately **he** received **his** sight, and followed Jesus in the way."

Matthew clearly says that there were two blind men. Mark says just as clearly that there was only one blind man and even provides his name, "Bartimaeus the son of Timaeus".

This contradiction is highly significant because Bible scholars say that the Gospel of Mark was one of the sources that was used by the writer of the Gospel of Matthew. They support this assertion by pointing out the numerous passages in Matthew that are almost word-for-word identical to those in Mark. Examples include Matthew 20:18-19 and Mark 10:33-34, Matthew 20:22-28 and Mark 10:39-45, Matthew 21:8-9 and Mark 11:8-10, and many others. This is only possible if the author of the Matthew had a copy of the Gospel of Mark in front of him while he was writing.

(continued on next page)

Since the author of the Gospel of Matthew had a copy of the Gospel of Mark when he was writing, the author of Matthew deliberately disagreed, in writing, with Mark's report. This contradiction goes far deeper than a simple difference of opinion between human authors. It even goes deeper than the obvious conclusion that the Bible cannot be perfect or inspired by God because it contradicts itself. This contradiction is convincing proof that the author of the Gospel of Matthew believed that the Gospel of Mark was wrong. In other words, **the author of the Gospel of Matthew did not believe the Gospel of Mark was inspired by God!** There is no other way to explain why the author of Matthew felt free to disagree with the Gospel of Mark's explicit record.

Some commentators argue that these were two separate events. The Bible itself disproves this argument for two reasons.

1 - The surrounding verses in Matthew and Mark match so closely that they have to be referring to the same sequence of the same events:

• Jesus predicted his death and resurrection in Matthew 20:17-19 and Mark 10:32-34

• James and John asked to sit with the glorified Jesus in Matthew 20:20-28 and Mark 10:35-45

• Matthew 20:29-34 and Mark 10:46-52 both say that this healing(s) happened as Jesus left Jericho with a great multitude

• Jesus' triumphal entry to Jerusalem immediately followed this healing, Matthew 21:1-9 and Mark 11:1-11.

2 - The texts of Matthew 20:29-34 and Mark 10:46-52 themselves provide convincing evidence that they are supposed to describe the same event.

• They match very closely, except for the number of blind men.

• The stories as reported simply do not make sense if they refer to two separate events. In both stories, the crowd told the blind man/men to be quiet before being healed and the formerly blind man/men followed Jesus after being healed. If these were two events, the crowd would have been extremely happy to see Jesus heal a blind person(s) a second time. Having recently seen a miraculous restoration of sight, the crowd would not have told any more blind people to be quiet; they would have encouraged them to go to Jesus so they could be healed. (If you doubt this, watch some "faith healing" services on television or attend a "faith healing" crusade. People who believe in faith healing love to see it done over and over again, or at least to convince themselves over and over again that they have seen it.) Besides, the man/men who was/were healed in the first healing would have been there to keep the crowd from "rebuking" any more blind people who asked to be healed.

Philip and Isaiah Got It Wrong 15 Times → An Evolving Myth

In Acts 8:32-35, the apostle Philip claimed that Jesus fulfilled a "prophecy" from Isaiah 53:7, which says, "He was oppressed, and he was afflicted, yet he opened not his mouth, he is brought as a lamb to the slaughter, and as a sheep before her shearers is dumb, so he openeth not his mouth".

Actually, though, the Bible says that Jesus spoke at least 15 times during his trial and crucifixion.

- John 18:20-21, to the high priest
- John 18:23, to the high priest
- Matthew 26:64, Mark 14:62, Luke 22:67-69, "Thou hast said, nevertheless I say unto you, Hereafter shall ye see the Son of man sitting on the right hand of power, and coming in the clouds of heaven".
- Luke 22:70, "Thou sayest I am" in front of the Sanhedrin
- John 18:34, "Sayest thou this thing yourself" to Pilate
- John 18:36, "My kingdom is not of this world" to Pilate
- Matthew 27:11, Mark 15:2, Luke 23:3, John 18:37, "Jesus said unto him, "Thou sayest," to Pilate
- John 19:11, "Thou couldest have no power against me except it were given thee", to Pilate
- Luke 23:28-31, several sentences to the daughters of Jerusalem
- John 19:26-27, "Woman behold thy son"
- Luke 23:34, "Father forgive them"
- Luke 23:43, Jesus spoke to a thief on the cross
- Matthew 27:46, Mark 15:34, "Eli, Eli, lama sabachthani"
- John 19:30,"It is finished"
- Matthew 27:50, Mark 15:37, Luke 23:46, "When he had cried again with a loud voice, yielded up the ghost"

This obviously disproves Isaiah's "prophecy", but the significance of this error goes far deeper, because this is one of those situations where you can actually see the "Jesus myth" evolving in the Bible itself. The first 8 chapters of Acts report events that supposedly occurred very shortly after Jesus' crucifixion. Acts 8:32-35 says that the Apostle Philip, an eyewitness to Jesus' crucifixion who was good friends with many other eyewitnesses, believed that Jesus did not speak during his trial and crucifixion. In addition, Philip believed that it was essential that Jesus not have spoken during his trial and crucifixion because it fulfilled an Old Testament prophecy about the Christ/Messiah.

But the Gospels, which were written a generation or more later, repeatedly say that Jesus did speak many times during his trial and crucifixion.

Many Resurrections Or Zero Resurrections?

Matthew 27:52-53 says that when Jesus died, "The graves were opened, and many bodies of the saints which slept arose and came out of the graves after his resurrection, and went into the holy city [Jerusalem], and appeared unto many."

Here is one miracle in the Gospels that, if it had really happened, would have been reported by other ancient historians and would provide a powerful evidence of the truth of the Bible's claims about miracles. Even Jewish and Pagan historians would have had to have taken notice of "many" people rising from their graves and being seen by "many" eyewitnesses living in Jerusalem, the capital city of Judea, a Roman province. They might have ascribed it to something other than God or Jesus, but they could not have ignored it.

Unfortunately for Bible believers, Matthew is the only writer from this period in history that mentions this large, albeit temporary, resurrection. Not one ancient historian mentions it; not even Josephus, the great first century Jewish historian who wrote dozens of chapters about this era in Jewish history.

The Gospels of Mark, Luke and John fail to mention it. So do the epistles of Paul, Peter, James, Jude and John, which expend enormous effort in trying to prove Jesus' divinity and resurrection. The fact that Jesus' death and resurrection was accompanied by the resurrections of many dead "saints", who "appeared to many", and that many of these witnesses would have still been alive if these books of the Bible were written when conservative Christians said they were written, would constitute powerful proof that there was something very uniquely supernatural about Jesus' death. But it is oddly absent from these books of the Bible.

If this mass resurrection really occurred, it is particularly strange that it would not be mentioned in the book of Acts. The first few chapters of Acts report events that allegedly happened very soon after Jesus' resurrection. The Apostles tried everything they could think of to persuade unbelievers to convert to Christianity, including numerous references to Old Testament prophecy, Jesus' crucifixion and resurrection, as well as speaking in tongues and performing miraculous healings. But not once does Acts report them saying, "How do you Pagans and Jews explain all of those people who raised from the dead in Jerusalem just a few weeks ago?" According to Acts 1:13, Matthew was definitely present during this time, but if he said anything about the mass resurrection the author of Luke did not think it was important enough to write down.

Matthew 27:52-53 contains another math error because it contradicts Hebrews 9:27, which says, "It is appointed to men once to die". These people died twice. They died and were buried. They were temporarily raised from the dead on the day that Jesus was crucified or resurrected. Then they died again some time later.

Zero Roommates In Jesus' Grave?

Matthew 27:57-60 says,

"When the even [evening] was come, there came a rich man of Arimathaea, named Joseph, who also himself was Jesus' disciple. He went to Pilate, and begged the body of Jesus. Then Pilate commanded the body to be delivered. And when Joseph had taken the body, he wrapped it in a clean linen cloth, and laid it in his own new tomb, which he had hewn out in the rock: and he rolled a great stone to the door of the sepulchre, and departed."

This story is repeated in Mark 15:43-47, Luke 23:50-53 and John 19:38-42 with minor variations.

Many apologists and commentators[8] claim that this is a fulfillment of a "prophecy" in Isaiah 53:9, "He made his grave with the wicked, and with the rich in his death".

If this short phrase in Isaiah is a prophecy is about Jesus, the Christ/Messiah, it makes 2 predictions, both of which are wrong.

Prediction #1: Christ would be buried with a wicked person. But Matthew 27:57 says that Joseph of Arimathea, "himself was Jesus' disciple". Mark 15:43 says that Joseph was, "an honorable counselor, which also waited for the Kingdom of God". Luke 23:50-51 says that he was, "a good man, and just ... who also himself waited for the kingdom of God". John 19:38 says that he was, "a disciple of Jesus". The Bible repeatedly says that Joseph of Arimathea was **not** "wicked".

Prediction #2: Christ would be buried with a rich person. But Matthew 27:60 says that this sepulcher was, "his [Joseph's] own new tomb". Luke 23:53 repeats this claim, "wherein never man before was laid". So does John 19:41, "a new sepulcher, wherein was never man yet laid". Not only did Jesus not make "his grave with ... the rich", he did **not** make his grave with anyone!

The resurrection of Jesus, if it occurred, was arguably the most important event in human history. But no one knows where or when it happened. Modern Christians claim two possible places. Catholics have built The Church of the Holy Sepulcher over one place. Many Protestants believe that Jesus' tomb was actually a place now called The Garden Tomb.

Not only do Christians disagree about where the resurrection happened, they disagree about when it happened. Easter for the Orthodox church is usually celebrated on a different date from the Easter celebrated by Catholics and Protestants. These disputes constitute powerful evidence against the historicity of Jesus' resurrection: believers cannot agree among themselves about the place and time of the one event which is the basis for all of their faith (1 Corinthians 15:17-19).

More Resurrected Math Errors

1 Corinthians 15:3-6 says, "I delivered unto you first of all that which I also received, how that Christ died for our sins according to the scriptures, And that he was buried, and that he rose again the third day according to the scriptures, And that he was seen of Cephas [Peter], then of the **twelve**. After that, he was seen of above **five hundred** brethren at once, of whom the greater part remain unto this present, but some are fallen asleep [died]."

This passage was allegedly written by the Apostle Paul, who did not convert to Christianity until some time after Jesus' resurrection and ascension. In this passage he assures us, however, that he "received" his information from credible sources, which the book of Acts says included the Apostles, who were eyewitnesses to the events that followed Jesus' resurrection. But there are two problems with this passage.

The first problem is that it contradicts all four Gospels and the book of Acts when it states that Jesus was seen by 12 Apostles. Those documents say that the risen Jesus only appeared to 11 Apostles because Judas Iscariot had betrayed Jesus and hanged himself. All of the "Pauline Epistles" are blissfully unaware of Judas Iscariot.

The second problem is the statement that Jesus,"was seen of above five hundred brethren at once". Although this is not contradicted by other parts of the Bible, they do not support it either. As with the mass resurrection reported on page 39 of this book, if this had actually happened it would have constituted extremely powerful evidence in favor of the historical validity of reports about Jesus' resurrection. Yet it is not mentioned anywhere else in the Bible.

As with the varying stories about Jesus' trial and crucifixion described on pages 38-39 above, 1 Corinthians 15:3-6 gives us two more myths about Jesus which are evolving before our eyes inside the Bible itself.

1 - Many conservative Bible scholars believe that 1 Corinthians was one of the first books of the New Testament to be written, since Paul is believed to have died around 62 CE. 1 Corinthians reports that the risen Jesus appeared to "the twelve". Later, all four Gospel writers claim with equal certitude that there were only eleven because of Judas' betrayal. Three Gospels specifically say, "the eleven": Matthew 28:16-17, Mark 16:14, Luke 24:9 and Luke 24:33.

2 - In 1 Corinthians, we are assured not only that Jesus appeared to over 500 "brethren" at one time, but also that most of these eyewitnesses were still alive at the time of writing. Yet these same eyewitnesses are strangely missing from the Gospels and Acts, as well as the non-Pauline epistles. As badly as Jesus' followers needed supporters and defenders in the book of Acts, not once is anyone quoted as saying, "I can show you over 500 eyewitnesses who saw the resurrected Christ", not even a few weeks after Pentecost, when hundreds of them would surely have been nearby.

Did 10 or 11 Apostles See Jesus On Easter?
More Evolution Of The Resurrection Myth . . .

As stated on the previous page, the Bible says that there were only 11 Apostles after Jesus' death and resurrection, but the story evolved further.

Most conservative Bible scholars believe that the Gospel of Luke was written many years before the Gospel of John. The Gospel of Luke says that 11 Apostles saw Jesus on the day of the resurrection. Luke 24:33-39 says that two men who had seen Jesus,

> "Rose up the same hour, and returned to Jerusalem, and found the **eleven** gathered together, and them that were with them, Saying, The Lord is risen indeed, and hath appeared to Simon. And they told what things were done in the way, and how he was known of them in breaking of bread. And as they thus spake, Jesus himself stood in the midst of them, and saith unto them, Peace be unto you. But they were terrified and affrighted, and supposed that they had seen a spirit. And he said unto them, Why are ye troubled? And why do thoughts arise in your hearts? Behold my hands and my feet, that it is I myself, handle me, and see; for a spirit hath not flesh and bones, as ye see me have."

But John 20:19-26 says only 10 disciples saw Jesus on the day of the resurrection. Thomas did not see Jesus until eight days later.

> "Then the same day at evening, being the first day of the week, when the doors were shut where the disciples were assembled for fear of the Jews, came Jesus and stood in the midst, and saith unto them, Peace be unto you. And when he had so said, he shewed unto them his hands and his side. Then were the disciples glad, when they saw the Lord. Then said Jesus to them again, Peace be unto you: as my Father hath sent me, even so send I you. And when he had said this, he breathed on them, and saith unto them, Receive ye the Holy Ghost, Whose soever sins ye remit, they are remitted unto them; and whose soever sins ye retain, they are retained. But **Thomas**, one of the twelve, called Didymus, **was not with them when Jesus came**. The other disciples therefore said unto him, We have seen the Lord. But he said unto them, Except I shall see in his hands the print of the nails, and put my finger into the print of the nails, and thrust my hand into his side, I will not believe. And **after eight days** again his disciples were within, and Thomas with them. Then came Jesus, the doors being shut, and stood in the midst."

When Did The Woman Pour The Ointment Over Jesus?

John 12:1-7 tells the story of a woman who poured expensive ointment on Jesus. "Then Jesus **six days before the Passover** came to Bethany ... Then took Mary a pound of ointment of spikenard, very costly, and anointed the feet of Jesus, and wiped his feet with her hair ... Then saith one of his disciples, Judas Iscariot, Simon's son, which should betray him, Why was not this ointment sold for three hundred pence, and given to the poor? This he said, not that he cared for the poor; but because he was a thief, and had the bag, and bare what was put therein. Then said Jesus, Let her alone: against the day of my burying hath she kept this." This was **before** Jesus' triumphal entry into Jerusalem, which was reported in John 12:12-19.

But Mark 14:1-8 says that this happened **after** Jesus' triumphal entry into Jerusalem (which Mark reported in chapter 11), "**After two days was the feast of the Passover,** and of unleavened bread ... And being in Bethany ... there came a woman having an alabaster box of ointment of spikenard very precious; and she brake the box, and poured it on his head. And there were some that had indignation within themselves, and said, Why was this waste of the ointment made? For it might have been sold for more than three hundred pence, and have been given to the poor ... And Jesus said, Let her alone; why trouble ye her? She hath wrought a good work on me ... she is come aforehand to anoint my body to the burying."

*   *   *

What Time Of Day Was Jesus Crucified?

John 19:14-16 says, "And it was the preparation of the Passover, and about the **sixth hour** [about noon], and he saith unto the Jews, Behold your King! But they cried out, Away with him, away with him, crucify him. ... Then delivered he him therefore unto them to be crucified. And they took Jesus, and led him away".

But Mark 15:25 says, "And it was the **third hour** [about 9 AM], and they crucified him".

*   *   *

One Or Two Angels?

Luke 24:4-7 says that **two** men told the women that Jesus had risen. John 20:12-13 says that **two** angels told them. Matthew 28:1-7 says that **one** angel told them. The Bible sometimes describes angels as having human form, but one does not equal two.

Chapter 3

"Historical" Math Mistakes

Conservative Bible believers are united in their assertion that the Bible is a historically accurate book. When the Bible claims that God sent an enormous pile of quail to feed the Hebrews, that God told the Israelites to slaughter huge numbers of unbelievers and that millions of Israelites sacrificed on a single altar, these reports are accepted as literally true without question.

As a preacher once said to me:

Rule #1: The Bible is the Infallible Word Of God

Rule #2: If you think anything is wrong with the Bible, see Rule #1

Historians use all available evidence to try to develop an accurate account of what actually happened. Biblical apologists subordinate all evidence to their conviction that the Bible is the Word of God; non-Biblical evidence which does not support this belief is regarded as false regardless of how well it is substantiated.

Many defenders of Christianity use what is euphemistically called "Presuppostional Apologetics" in support of their beliefs. The foundational belief of Presuppostional Apologetics is that you must accept Jesus' divinity by faith before you will understand the evidence for Jesus' divinity. In their minds, evidence is literally irrelevant because if God wants to save you then he doesn't need evidence, and if God doesn't want to save you then no amount of evidence will make any difference.

This idea has Biblical support. Romans 1:17 says, "The just shall live by faith", not evidence. 2 Corinthians 5:7 says, "We walk by faith, not by sight". John 20:29 quotes Jesus as saying, "Blessed are they that have **not** seen, and yet have believed". See also Appendix 2, "Blind Faith".

100 Bible Math Mistakes uses the Bible itself to evaluate its own historicity. It assumes, for the sake of argument only, that the numbers presented in the Bible are what the Bible claims that they are. The first time I studied this, it was much more than an assumption. I was a full-time ministerial student working on a Master of Divinity degree in a conservative Christian seminary. I was completely convinced of the absolute truth and infallibility of the Bible and I studied very hard so that I could prove it to other people. Because the evidence from the Bible itself was overwhelmingly against this belief (including but not limited to mathematical and historical evidence), I became an Atheist while I was studying to be a minister.

Even a superficial examination of the mathematics of the "historical" books of the Bible reveals that they are more hysterical than historical. Time and again, even simple things do not add up. Many of these errors and contradictions strike at the heart of essential Christian beliefs.

Moses' Ghost Writer's 450-Year Oops

Genesis 36:31 says, "These are the kings that reigned in the land of Edom, before there reigned any king over the children of Israel".

The Old Testament claims that Moses wrote the first 5 books of the Bible, also called the Pentateuch or "The Law", in Joshua 8:32 and many places in the Pentateuch itself.

In the New Testament, Jesus himself claimed that Moses wrote the Old Testament Law in John 1:17 and 7:19. The Apostle Paul made the same claim in Romans 10:5. The belief that Moses wrote the Pentateuch is so widely accepted among Christian conservatives that I have never met one who does not believe it.

If Moses really wrote Genesis 36:31, this verse makes no sense because he died hundreds of years before Saul was made the first king of Israel. Joshua lived for 30 years after Moses died, according to Joshua 14:7-10 and 24:29. After Joshua died, God, "gave unto them judges about the space of **four hundred and fifty years**, until Samuel the prophet", according to Acts 13:20. Samuel anointed Saul as king in 1 Samuel 9:15-10:1.

Throughout the entire lives of Joshua and all of the Judges of Israel (except Samuel, the very last Judge) Israel never had a king. If this verse was really written by Moses, the Israelites who read it would have shaken their heads and said the Hebrew equivalent of, "Why the heck is that in there? We have never had a king!". They would have said this for almost five hundred years before Saul was even born - during the leadership of Joshua, and the Hebrew judges Othniel, Ehud, Shamgar, Deborah, Barak, Gideon, Tolah, Jair, Jephthah, Ibzan, Elon, Abdon, Samson or Eli.

In the lifetime of Moses, the statement, "before there reigned any king over the children of Israel", would be as out of place as if Christopher Columbus had written that something had happened, "before the United States elected their first President". Any historian who encounters such a statement would be compelled by the evidence and by professional standards to conclude that the document is a forgery because it claims to have been written by a person who died hundreds of years before an event it refers to.

Genesis 36:31 is very powerful evidence that at least portions of the book of Genesis were not written until centuries after the death of Moses. If so, Joshua, Jesus and Paul were all wrong.

.

God Sadistically Killed Trillions Of Animals For No Reason

One of the most famous Bible stories is the story of Noah's Ark and the worldwide Flood. The evidence against the Flood is overwhelming, a fact that has been explained very well in many other books. Creationists' faith in a literal interpretation of Genesis causes them to reject those books and those facts a priori.

So, for the sake of argument only, we will assume that The Flood happened like the Bible says it did, assume that the, "wickedness of man was great in the earth, and that every imagination of the thoughts of his heart was only evil continually" (Genesis 6:5), and assume that these evil human hearts gave God legitimate reasons to kill almost the entire human race. What does this story tell us about God?

If the Bible-God is all-powerful, he can kill as many humans as he wants to without harming a single animal. In Exodus chapters 11-12, for example, God killed all of the firstborn humans in Egypt in a single night. He had time to check for sheep's blood on every door so that he would not kill a single Hebrew, and even knew how to identify and kill only the firstborn even if there were many other Egyptians in the same house. This is one of many examples in the Bible where God killed large numbers of carefully selected people. Other examples include 1 Samuel 6:19, 2 Samuel chapter 24, Numbers 16:49, Numbers 25:1-9 and 2 Kings 19:35.

So it was completely unnecessary and actually quite cruel for God to flood the earth so that, "All flesh died that moved upon the earth, both of fowl, and of cattle, and of beast, and of every creeping thing that creepeth upon the earth, and every man. All in whose nostrils was the breath of life, of all that was in the dry land, died. And every living substance was destroyed which was upon the face of the ground, both man, and cattle, and the creeping things, and the fowl of the heaven; and they were destroyed from the earth", as it says in Genesis 7:21-23.

God claims in Proverbs 12:10 that, "A righteous man regardeth the life of his beast, but the tender mercies of the wicked are cruel". But in Genesis, it was God who was cruel. What had all of those animals done to deserve death?

Psalm 145:16 claims, "Thou [God] openest thine hand and satisfiest the desire of every living thing". But in Genesis chapter 7, all of those animals desired air and God drowned them.

If you deliberately drown a horse or a dog, it is a felony in most civilized nations. If God drowns enormous numbers of them for no reason, it is a miracle.

It gets worse, because it didn't solve the problem. After the flood, Genesis 8:21 quotes God as saying, "the imagination of man's heart is evil from his youth", just like Genesis 6:5 (see above). So the Flood did not make human hearts or imaginations less evil. If God was really all-knowing, he would have known this before he sent the flood and unnecessarily drowned those trillions of animals.

God Plans To Kill Trillions More Animals For No Reason

Some of the most famous Bible prophecies predict that God will destroy the entire Earth and replace it with a new, improved Earth. 2 Peter 3:10 says, "The heavens shall pass away with a great noise, and the elements shall melt with fervent heat, the earth also and the works that are therein shall be burned up". Nahum 1:5 says, "The hills melt, and the earth is burned at his presence, yea the world and all that dwell therein". Psalm 75:3 says, "The earth and all the inhabitants thereof are dissolved". Psalm 97:5 says, "The hills melted like wax at the presence of the Lord".

This immolation is scheduled to occur after various environmental disasters described in the book of Revelation:

• Revelation 8:7 says, "The first angel sounded, and there followed hail and fire mingled with blood, and they were cast upon the earth, and the third part of trees was burnt up and all green grass was burnt up".

• Revelation 8:8-9 says, "The second angel sounded, and as it were a great mountain burning with fire was cast into the sea, and the third part of the sea became blood. And the third part of the creatures which were in the sea, and had life, died."

• Revelation 16:3 says, "The second angel poured out his vial upon the sea, and it became as the blood of a dead man, and every living soul died in the sea."

• Revelation 16:12 says, "The sixth angel poured out his vial upon the great river Euphrates and the water thereof was dried up."

• Revelation 16:17-20 says, "The seventh angel poured out his vial into the air ... and there was a great earthquake, such as was not since men were upon the earth, so mighty an earthquake, and so great ... And every island fled away, and the mountains were not found."

These cataclysms would surely cause enormous carnage among land animals who had done nothing to offend God. The Bible also explicitly says that all life in the seas will die, including highly intelligent "living souls" like dolphins and whales. Then God plans to incinerate the entire earth and everything on it.

All of this is completely unnecessary. Omnipotent God can smite carefully selected people with painful illnesses, as he did in Deuteronomy 28:28 and 1 Samuel 5:6-12, he can get Satan to do his dirty work for him as he did in the book of Job, or he can simply kill as many carefully selected humans he wants to, as described on the preceding page of this book. He can do all of this without harming a single animal, if he is really omnipotent.

God claims in Proverbs 12:10 that, "A righteous man regardeth the life of his beast, but the tender mercies of the wicked are cruel". But if the apocalyptic prophecies of the Bible are true, God will cruelly, senselessly and unnecessarily kill even more animals than he did in Genesis.

The Birth of Isaac And The Genesis Chronology

The Bible waxes eloquently about what a great miracle it was for God to make Abraham and Sarah bear a son, Isaac, when Abe was 100 years old and Sarah was 90, and what great faith it took for them to believe that God would do so. This story is reported in Genesis chapters 15-21. It is referenced in Romans 4:1-5 and Hebrews 11:11-12.

A brief examination of the book of Genesis, however, shows that having a baby at these supposedly elderly ages would not have been unusual at that time in Bible "history", for the simple reason that people allegedly lived much longer. Genesis 23:1 says that Sarah lived for 37 years after giving birth to Isaac, so she would have been quite a bit more vivacious than a non-Biblical 90-year old woman would be even today. Genesis 25:7 says that Abraham lived to be 175 years old. He continued to be virile after Sarah's death, which occurred when he was 137 years old, because Genesis 25:1-2 says that after Sarah died, "Abraham took a wife, and her name was Keturah. And she bare him Zimran, and Jokshan, and Medan, and Midian, and Ishbak, and Shuah". Abe's sperm remained fully functional well into his 140's.

The most definitive proof that Abe and Sarah were not too old to have children comes from doing some simple math on the genealogies in Genesis. This also gives us some good reasons not to believe the Genesis chronology (or mythology), because if these ages are correct, there are some things that just don't make sense.

Table 1 lists the Bible's years of birth and death for the Genesis patriarchs from Noah through Isaac, relative to the year of the Flood.

If Genesis is historically accurate, then the following direct ancestors of Abraham were **still alive** at the time that Isaac was born:

- Abe's father Terah, age 170
- Abe's great-grandfather Serug, age 229
- Abe's great-great-great-great grandfather Eber, age 325
- Abe's great-great-great-great-great grandfather Salah, age 355
- Abe's great-great-great-great-great-great grandfather Arphaxad, age 390
- Abe's great-great-great-great-great-great-great grandfather Shem, age 490

If you have a living direct ancestor who is almost 500 years old, three living direct ancestors who are 300-400 years old and two more living direct ancestors who are 170-229 years old, then it will surely come as no surprise that you have fertile gonads at the age of 90-100. Sarah was less than one-fifth the age of Abraham's still living 7-times-great grandfather Shem, and less than one-third the age of three of Abraham's other living direct ancestors, Eber, Salah and Arphaxad.

(continued on next page)

Table 1
Genesis Patriarchs From Noah To Isaac

Name	Father's Age When He Was Born	# Years After Flood When He Was Born	Total # Years Lived	# Years After The Flood When He Died	Age When Isaac Was Born	# Years Lived After Isaac Was Born	Reference
Noah	-	600 yrs before	950	350	Deceased	-	Genesis 7:11, 9:29
Shem	500	98 yrs before	598	500	490	108	Genesis 5:32, 11:10-11
Arphaxad	100	2	438	440	390	48	Genesis 11:10-13
Salah	35	37	433	470	355	78	Genesis 11:12-15
Eber	30	67	464	531	325	139	Genesis 11:14-17
Peleg	34	101	239	340	Deceased	-	Genesis 11:16-19
Reu	30	131	239	370	Deceased	-	Genesis 11:18-21
Serug	32	163	230	393	229	1	Genesis 11:20-23
Nahor	30	193	148	341	Deceased	-	Genesis 11:22-25
Terah	29	222	205	427	170	35	Genesis 11:24-26, 11:32
Abraham	70	292	175	467	100	75	Genesis 11:26-32, 25:7
Isaac	100	392	180	572	-	180	Genesis 21:5, 35:28

(continued on next page)

The Birth of Isaac & The Genesis Chronology (continued from preceding pages)

Noah died when Abraham was 58 years old, if the Bible is correct, and three of Abe's ancestors - Shem, Salah and Eber - actually died after Abe died. Yet the Bible contains no hint of contact between him and any of his ancestors, except his father Terah.

Abraham lived in a very patriarchal society. Shem had actually heard the voice of God in Genesis 9:1-16. The counsel of a sage who had seen the miraculous Flood, knew what God's voice sounded like, had hundreds of years of experience and was directly related to him, would have been extremely valuable to Abraham in his many adventures and spiritual struggles. Abraham would have also been obligated to seek Shem's guidance on major parenting decisions. But there is no mention of Abraham asking Shem any important questions like, "Great Grandpa Shem, should I cut off part of my son's penis?" or "Great Grandpa Shem, God told you not to shed human blood (Genesis 9:6), but God just told me to make my son a burnt offering. Did God ever tell you to do anything like that?"

If you had met the star witnesses of the Genesis Flood - Noah and Shem - and those people happened to be your immediate family, or even if you merely knew that they were alive at the same time you were, it would not take much faith to make you believe that God would help you impregnate your wife, particularly if you were 1/5 their age.

There is nothing in the Bible to indicate that this genealogy and the lifespans that go with it should not be taken literally. Theologians such as Ussher, Scofield and others believed that these ages were so mathematically precise that they used them to help calculate the year in which God created the universe as 4004 BCE, a date which is still accepted by many conservative Christian leaders and Creationists. The Jewish calendar says this date is 3761 BCE. (The fact that Jewish and Christian Old Testament scholars disagree about the Biblical date of creation is yet another example of the Bible contradicting itself about something that is mathematically very important.)

It is beyond the scope of this book to discuss all of the fallacies of Biblical Creationism. There are many excellent books that do so very well. But Table 1 and Graph 1 clearly illustrate one insurmountable fallacy of a historical interpretation of the book of Genesis: the ages of the post-flood Patriarchs in Genesis clearly contradict key elements of the story of Abraham if they are interpreted as actual history, and vice versa. If you prove that the Genesis timeline is invalid, you prove that the creation of the universe could not have occurred at the point in time that the Bible says it did.

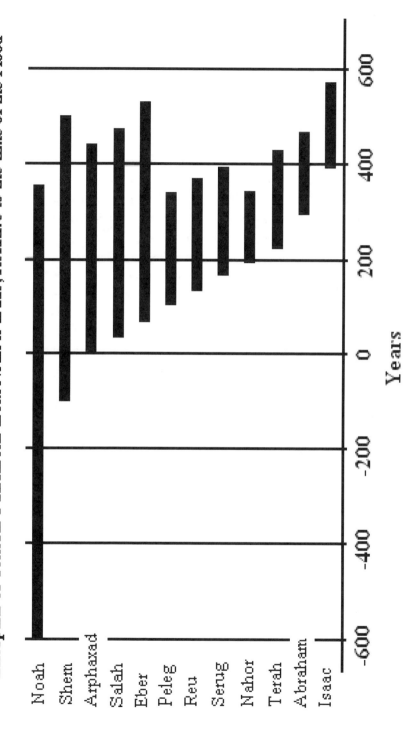

Lifespans of Genesis Patriarchs from Noah to Isaac, Relative to the time of the Flood

Were The Israelites In Egypt 255, 350 or 430 years?

Exodus 12:40-41 says, "Now the sojourning of the children of Israel, who dwelt in Egypt, was **four hundred and thirty years**. And it came to pass at the end of the **four hundred and thirty years**, even the selfsame day it came to pass, that all the hosts of the Lord went out from the land of Egypt". This passage very clearly states that the Israelites were in Egypt for exactly **430** years, accurate to "even the selfsame day". But other Bible passages say that it was a very different number of years.

The book of Exodus provides a timeline for Moses and his ancestors:

- Moses was 80 years old at the time the Israelites left Egypt - Exodus 7:7
- Moses' father, Amram, lived 137 years - Exodus 6:20
- Amram's father, Kohath, lived 133 years - Exodus 6:16-18
- Kohath went to Egypt in Genesis 46:8-11

The Bible presents this genealogy and timeline as literal history. If we make the most generous possible assumptions, that Amram and Moses were each born in the year that their father died and Kohath was a baby when he went to Egypt, we get a maximum of 80 + 137 + 133 = **350** years that the Israelites were in Egypt.

Galatians 3:16-17 contradicts both of the above calculations, "To Abraham and his seed were the promises made ... the law, which was **four hundred and thirty years after**". Galatians 3:16 is referring to promises that God made to Abraham in Genesis 22:18. Galatians 3:17 is referring to Exodus 12:40-41 and subsequent chapters, which say that Israel received God's Law shortly after leaving Egypt.

To quantify the contradiction in Galatians, calculate the years between the events in Genesis chapter 22 and Kohath's entry into Egypt. We will estimate that Isaac was 15 years old in Genesis 22, because Genesis 22:5 says that he was a "lad" and Genesis 22:6 says that he was big enough to carry, "the wood of the burnt offering". (A "lad" carrying his own funeral pyre! How bizarre!) Using a somewhat higher or lower age for Isaac won't make much difference, because Galatians contradicts Exodus by a large margin. Here is the time line:

Years	Event
0	God's promise & Abraham's sacrifice of Isaac - Genesis Chapter 22
22	Sarah died, aged 127 - Genesis 23:1
45	Jacob/Israel born. Isaac 60 years old - Genesis 25:26
165	Isaac died, aged 180 - Genesis 35:28-29
175	Jacob/Israel, aged 130, entered Egypt with Kohath - Genesis 47:9

So the Bible clearly says that 175 years passed between God's promise to Abe and the Israelites' arrival in Egypt. If you subtract these years, you get 430 - 175 = **255** years that the Israelites would have been in Egypt, according to Galatians 3:16-17.

Trillions Of Quail Bones Mysteriously Missing

In Numbers chapter 11, the Hebrews got tired of eating mannah and so they asked for meat. Numbers 11:31-32 reports God's response:

"There went forth a wind from the Lord and brought quails from the sea, and let them fall by the camp, as it were a day's journey on this side, and as it were a day's journey on the other side, round about the camp, and as it were **two cubits high** upon the face of the earth. And the people stood up all that day, and all that night, and all the next day, and they gathered the quails. He that gathered least gathered ten homers. And they spread them all abroad for themselves round about the camp."

It would have been an enormous volume of birds. This passage claims that this pile of dead birds were "two cubits" deep and "a day's journey" broad on both sides of the camp of the Israelites. A cubit is the distance from a person's elbow to the tip of their fingers, about 1.5 feet. The length of "a day's journey" is not given, but most nomadic people can easily travel over 10 miles in a day. So, if the Bible is mathematically accurate, this mass of dead quails was 3 feet high with a radius of at least 10 miles. The formula for calculating volume is:

Height * Radius Squared * π = Volume

3 feet * (10 miles * 5280 feet per mile)^2 * 3.14 = 26,261,452,800

That is over 26 billion cubic feet of dead birds. Numbers 11:33 says that the Hebrews did not eat many of them because, "While the flesh was yet between their teeth, ere it was chewed, the wrath of the Lord was kindled against the people, and the Lord smote the people with a very great plague"[1].

This is one of those rare miracles that would have left abundant physical evidence that could easily be found and examined. If this miracle really occurred, there would be:

• An enormous mass of bird bones
• Covering over 300 square miles (10 miles squared * π)
• All from birds of the same taxonomic family
• Physically located in the Sinai peninsula or Negev desert
• Which could be carbon-14 dated to approximately 3500 years ago.

This entire region is quite dry, so many of these bones would have survived to the present day. But no such pile exists, nor are there any historical references to such a pile after the events reported in Numbers chapter 11. If this had really happened, the evidence for it would be overwhelming. Instead, the absence of this evidence constitutes overwhelming evidence against the historicity of Numbers chapter 11.

God Ordered > 3,000,000 Violations Of "Thou Shalt Not Murder"

All civilized societies agree that murder is one of the most heinous crimes that someone can commit. Some form of legal prohibition against murder was present in ancient civilizations, many of which pre-date the Old Testament by many centuries. The Bible echoes this prohibition. Exodus 20:13 and Deuteronomy 5:17 say, "Thou Shalt Not Kill", which many modern Bibles translate as, "Thou shalt not murder".

Nevertheless, the history of God's followers is awash with rivers of innocent human blood - in holy wars, persecutions, witch hunts, crusades and pogroms - perpetrated by Hebrews and Christians who believed that God told them to murder people whose beliefs they disapproved of. In Deuteronomy 20:16-18, God commanded,

> "Of the cities of these people, which the Lord thy God doth give thee for an inheritance, thou shalt save alive nothing that breatheth. But thou shalt utterly destroy them; namely, the Hittites, and the Amorites, the Canaanites, and the Perizzites, the Hivites, and the Jebusites; as the Lord thy God hath command- ed thee. That they teach you not to do after all their abominations, which they have done unto their gods; so should ye sin against the Lord your God."

Although the Bible makes multitudes of claims that God is merciful and just, there are some particularly **un**merciful and **un**just things about this command:

• **Genocide:** Utter extermination of "everything that breathes", including innocent women, children, babies, disabled and elderly. Embryos and fetuses were destroyed, even though Romans 9:11 says that they had not done "any good or evil".

• **Repentance Not Allowed:** The Bible repeatedly claims that God wants everyone to be saved. But in this passage, these people would not be allowed to con- vert to Judaism. They were to be exterminated.

• **Preemptive murder:** These people were not to be killed because of sins they had committed. They were to be killed because of things they hadn't even done - to prevent them from teaching Hebrews, "to do after all their abominations". Why was omnipotent God so threatened by little heathen babies that he had to kill them?

• **Inescapable Sins:** If the Hebrews obeyed God's commands in Exodus 20:13 and Deuteronomy 5:17, they would violate God's command in Deuteronomy 20:16-18. They were literally damned if you do and damned if you don't.

God commanded many similar genocides in the Bible, including but not lim- ited to the Midianites in Numbers 31:6-35, Amalekites in 1 Samuel 15:3-8 , people in the kingdom of Bashan in Numbers 21:33-35, people in the kingdom of Hormah in Numbers 21:3, people in the kingdom of Heshbon in Deuteronomy 2:30-34 and people in the kingdoms of the Geshurites and Gezrites in 1 Samuel 27:8-11.

(continued on next page)

God's followers enthusiastically carried out these genocides. As King David said in Psalm 58:10, "The righteous shall rejoice when he seeth the vengeance, he shall wash his feet in the blood of the wicked". Examples of the slaughter include:

- **Hormah,** "utterly destroyed them and their cities", Numbers 21:3
- **Midian,** all males and all non-virgin females, Numbers 31:6-35
- **Heshbon,** "utterly destroyed the men and the women and the little ones", Deuteronomy 2:30-34 and 3:6
- **Bashan,** "we utterly destroyed ... men, women and children of every city", Deuteronomy 3:3-6.
- **Ai, Makkedah, Libnah, Lachish, Gezer, Eglon, Hebron, Debir, Gibeon, "from Kadesh-barnea even unto Gaza", Hazor, Madon, Shimron, Achshaph, Amorites, Hittites, Perizzites, Jebusites** "there was not any left to breathe", Joshua Chapters 10-12
- **Amalekites,** "Slay both man and woman, infant and suckling .... utterly destroyed all the people with ... the sword", 1 Samuel 15:3-8
- **Geshurites, Gezrites, Amalekites,** "David smote ... left neither man nor woman alive", 1 Samuel 27:8-11
- **Jerusalem,** "the lame and the blind" 2 Samuel 5:7-9

Deuteronomy 7:1-7 provides enough information to estimate how many people were killed by the Israelites. Verse 1 says that the nations that the Israelites conquered were, "seven nations greater and mightier than thou". Verse 7 says that the Israelites were, "fewest of all people".

So the Israelites killed at least enough non-Israelites to exceed the size of their own population. Numbers 26:51 and Exodus 38:26 say that there were 601,730 or 603,550 Israelite men. Since there would have been about the same number of women, and conservatively estimating 3 children per family, this would mean that there were at least 3 million Israelites.

If the Bible is historically accurate, the Israelites slaughtered at least <u>3 million people</u>; one of the biggest genocides in recorded history was committed by God's followers at his command.

Some Christians argue that the Bible's stories about God's martyrs are evidence that the Bible is true. But relatively few Jehovah/Jesus worshippers were martyred in the Bible: Abel, John the Baptist, Stephen, James the brother of John, and possibly 85 priests in 1 Samuel Chapter 22. The Bible says, however, that literally millions of people were martyred because they believed in Baal, Molech, Chemosh, Ashteroth and other pagan deities. If theological truth is determined by body count, God and Jesus lose by a landslide according to their own book.

How Many Items Were Kept In the Ark Of The Covenant?

Hebrews 9:4 says, "The Ark of the Covenant overlaid round about with gold, wherein was the golden pot that had manna, and Aaron's rod that budded, and the tables of the covenant".

But 2 Kings 8:9 says, "There was nothing in the ark save the two tables of stone, which Moses put there at Horeb, when the Lord made a covenant with the children of Israel, when they came out of the land of Egypt". 2 Chronicles 5:10 says the same thing almost word-for-word.

Some apologists argue that the manna and rod were placed in the Ark and later removed. But 2 Samuel 6:6-7 says that touching the Ark brought instant death, which is why they carried it on poles without touching it. 1 Samuel 6:13-19 says that simply looking inside the Ark caused God to kill over 50,000 people. So it would have been impossible for anyone to add anything to or remove anything from the Ark.

Once again, we see evidence of an evolving myth in the Bible. In ancient times, the belief that the Ark of the Covenant existed and that it contained actual artifacts from the time of the Exodus was regarded as powerful evidence for the historical truth of the Bible. This "evidence" was accepted by faith even though it was hidden behind curtains in the temple so no one could see it except the high priest, according to 2 Chronicles 5:9 and Hebrews 9:3-4, and nobody could look at these items without God killing them. By the time the book of Hebrews was written, it was impossible to verify what had been in the Ark because 2 Chronicles 36:18 says that the Babylonians took it around 593-586 BCE. There is no credible record of it after that time.

The Ark of the Covenant[2]

The Amorites Just Wouldn't Die

The Bible says that the Amorites were repeatedly exterminated. But the Israelites had to fight them again and again.

According to Deuteronomy 31:4, the Amorites had two kings: Sihon and Og. In Deuteronomy 2:32-34, "Sihon came out against us, he and all his people, to fight at Jahaz. And the Lord our God delivered him before us; and we smote him, and his sons, and all his people. And we took all his cities at that time, and utterly destroyed the men, and the women, and the little ones, of every city, we left none to remain." Deuteronomy 3:1-6 says, "Og the king of Bashan came out against us, he and all his people, to battle at Edre ... we utterly destroyed them, as we did unto Sihon king of Heshbon, utterly destroying the men, women, and children, of every city." At that point, there were precisely **zero** living Amorites, if the Bible is accurate.

But the Israelites had to fight the Amorites again in Joshua chapter 11. This time the Amorites were allied with other pagan nations. Joshua 11:14-15 assures us that the Israelites, "neither left they any to breathe. As the Lord commanded Moses his servant, so did Moses command Joshua, and so did Joshua; he left nothing undone of **all** that the Lord commanded Moses". This is a reference to Deuteronomy 20:16-17, "Of the cities of these people ... thou shalt save alive nothing that breatheth, But thou shalt utterly destroy them; namely, the Hittites, and the **Amorites**, the Canaanites, and the Perizzites, the Hivites, and the Jebusites; as the Lord thy God hath commanded thee". Once again, we are down to **zero** breathing Amorites.

But Judges 1:34 says, "The Amorites forced the children of [the Israelite tribe] Dan into the mountain, for they would not suffer [allow] them to come down to the valley". Not bad for an extinct ethnic group. The Amorites continued to exist at least until the time of chapter 9 in the book of Ezra, around 460 BCE.

* * *

Midian Makes A Miraculous Recovery

Numbers chapter 31 says that the Israelites killed all of the Midianite males and non-virgin females, but they kept 32,000 female virgins for themselves, i.e., as slaves and concubines. This would have effectively wiped out Midian as a nation and ethnic group, because these girls were deprived of property, family and freedom, then assimilated into the male-controlled society of their masters.

Just a few generations later, however, Judges 6:1-6 says that the Midianites had grown so strong that, "the hand of Midian prevailed against Israel" and "Israel was greatly impoverished because of the Midianites".

Perhaps They Should Drive A Stake Into Every Canaanite Heart

Time and again, the Old Testament says that the Israelites killed all of the Canaanites, yet somehow the Canaanites kept coming back.

The first extermination was in Numbers 21:2-3, "Israel vowed a vow unto the Lord, and said, If thou wilt indeed deliver this people into my hand, then I will utterly destroy their cities. And the Lord hearkened to the voice of Israel, and delivered up the Canaanites; and they utterly destroyed them and their cities." The number of living Canaanites at that time was precisely **zero**, according to the Bible.

Although they had already "utterly destroyed" the Canaanites, the Israelites had to fight them again in the book of Joshua. The Bible claims that the Canaanites were wiped out again, because Joshua chapters 10 and 11 describe a complete slaughter and then Joshua 11:15 says, "As the Lord commanded Moses his servant, so did Moses command Joshua, and so did Joshua; he left nothing undone of all that the Lord commanded Moses". This would include Deuteronomy 20:16-17, where God commanded, "Of the cities of these people, which the Lord thy God doth give thee for an inheritance, thou shalt save alive nothing that breatheth. But thou shalt utterly destroy them; namely, ... the Canaanites ... as the Lord thy God hath commanded thee".

The above passages leave no room for doubt. Every Canaanite man, woman, child and infant had been massacred. Joshua 11:23 re-states the obvious, "So Joshua took the whole land, according to all that Jehovah said unto Moses; and Joshua gave it for an inheritance unto Israel according to their divisions by their tribes". So does Joshua 21:43, "The Lord gave unto Israel all the land which he sware to give unto their fathers; and they possessed it, and dwelt therein", which they had no difficulty doing because they had killed everyone who had lived there. The Bible clearly and repeatedly that the Canaanite ethnic group was again reduced to **zero**.

But the reportedly twice-exterminated Canaanites stayed around for over a thousand years afterwards. Joshua 13:1-5 says, "The Lord said unto him [Joshua], Thou art old and stricken in years, and there remaineth yet very much land to be possessed. This is the land that yet remaineth", including "Sihor, which is before Egypt, even unto the borders of Ekron northward, which is counted to the Canaanite" and "from the south, all the land of the Canaanites".

Judges 3:1-5 says, "Now these are the nations which the Lord left ....the Canaanites". Ezra 9:1 says that the Canaanites were still around when the Israelites returned from Babylon around 450-460 BCE. Matthew 10:4 and Mark 3:18 say that "Simon the Canaanite" was one of Jesus' Apostles.

God "Takes Care Of" > 30,000 Widows And Orphans

The Bible repeatedly claims that God takes especially good care of widows and orphans. Psalm 68:5 says that God is "father of the fatherless". Psalm 10:14 says that God is, "helper of the fatherless". Psalm 146:9 says that God, "relieveth the fatherless and widow". James 1:27 says, "Pure religion and undefiled before God and the Father is this, To visit the fatherless and widows in their affliction".

The Bible does report that God was kind to a few widows and orphans. For example, 2 Kings 4:1-7 says that the prophet Elisha miraculously prevented two orphans from being sold into slavery. 1 Timothy 5:9-11 says that the church should take care of widows who are 60 years old or older, but only if they have raised children and "washed the saints' feet". (At that time, most people died before their 40th birthday.)

But the vast majority of widows and orphans mentioned in the Bible did not fare so well. As previously described in "God Ordered > 3,000,000 Violations Of 'Thou Shalt Not Murder'", the Israelites killed all of the men in the armies of the pagan ethnic groups living in the Promised Land. This created millions of defenseless widows and orphans. The closest thing to "help" or "relief" that was shown to these widows and orphans was a quick death under a Hebrew sword.

One Bible story deserves special mention. Numbers 31:1-2 says, "The Lord spake unto Moses, saying, Avenge the children of Israel of the Midianites". So the Israelite army defeated the Midianite army and killed all of the men, creating a large number of widows and orphans, whom they did not kill until Moses rebuked them.

Numbers 31:14-18 says, "Moses was wroth with the officers of the host, with the captains over thousands, and captains over hundreds, which came from the battle. And Moses said unto them, Have ye saved all the women alive? Behold, these caused the children of Israel, through the counsel of Balaam, to commit trespass against the Lord in the matter of Peor, and there was a plague among the congregation of the Lord. Now therefore kill every male among the little ones, and kill every woman that hath known man by lying with him. But all the women children, that have not known a man by lying with him, keep alive for yourselves."

God did not explain why male virgins were guilty of this capital offense but female virgins were not. Nor did he explain how women or children could have had anything to do with leading the Israelites astray in a male-dominated society. Nor did he explain how, if people really have free will, anyone except the Israelites themselves could have, "caused the children of Israel ... to commit trespass against the Lord".

Whatever God's reasons were, his command was dutifully carried out. Numbers 31:35 says that 32,000 female orphan virgins were spared, so about that many male orphan virgins, plus many thousands of widowed mothers, were slaughtered.

Over A Thousand Sacrifices Every Day, But Only One Altar

The book of Leviticus contains detailed instructions for ritual sacrifices which each individual Israelite was required to do on numerous occasions:

1. Firstborn child - Exodus 13:2-15, Exodus 34:20
2. Firstborn ass - Exodus 13:13
3. Individual sin through ignorance - Leviticus 4:27-34, Numbers 15:27-28
4. Swearing - Leviticus 5:1-7
5. Touching any unclean person or thing - Leviticus 5:2-7
6. Theft or fraud - Leviticus 6:2-7
7. Peace offering to fulfill a vow - Leviticus 22:21

Items 1-7 above make it clear that every Israelite man would have to make several sacrifices each year. Women were also commanded to make specific sacrifices, e.g., Leviticus 15:25-30. The Israelites had good reasons to take these Laws very seriously because God very frequently killed people who didn't do what he said.

These animals were killed in elaborate rituals that required:

• Killing and dismembering each animal - Leviticus 1:6-9
• Washing some of the parts - Leviticus 1:9
• Sprinkling their blood in various places - Leviticus 1:11 and 4:6
• Burning certain parts or even the entire animal on an altar - Exodus 29:18

Exodus 38:26 says that there were 603,550 adult Israelite men at this time. If we assume only 1 sacrifice per Israelite man per year, that is about 600,000 sacrifices per year, or about 1600 per day. This would be no problem if there were large numbers of priests and altars.

But Leviticus 1:7-8 and 17:1-5, Numbers 4:15 and 2 Chronicles 26:16-21 all say that only Aaron and his sons could offer sacrifices. Although "son" may mean "descendant", the Bible explicitly says that at the time of Leviticus 10:16, Aaron had only two living "sons", Eleazar and Ithamar. So whether Eleazar and Ithamar were sons, grandsons or great grandsons, there were only two of them and so available manpower was severely limited. Eleazar did eventually have a son, Phinehas, so maybe there were 4 priests who could perform sacrifices for 600,000 Hebrew men and hundreds of thousands of Hebrew women during the time of the books of Exodus, Leviticus, Numbers and Deuteronomy, while they wandered in the desert for 40 years.

The most severe limitation, however, was that there was only one altar. If you sacrificed on any other altar, Leviticus 10:1-2 and Numbers 18:6-8 required that you be put to death. God was serious about this. Numbers 3:4 says that Aaron's other two sons, Nadab and Abihu, "offered strange fire before the Lord" so God killed them.

(continued on next page)

Exodus chapter 38 gives very detailed instructions for construction of the altar, including the requirement that the surface area of the top of the altar be only 5 x 5 cubits, i.e., about 7.5 x 7.5 feet.

The Old Testament Altar of Jehovah[3]

So there was only 1 altar. Its top, where the sacrifices were made was a square measuring 7.5 feet on each side. On this altar, no more than 4 priests supposedly performed over 1,600 ritual sacrifices each day. Assuming that the priests worked around the clock on rotating shifts. There are

24 * 60 = 1440 minutes in a day

1440 / 1600 = 0.90 minute per sacrifice

0.90 * 60 = 54 seconds per sacrifice

Anyone who can barbecue knows from personal experience that it takes a lot longer than 54 seconds to burn even part of an animal. Although Deuteronomy 12:27 allowed for some of the sacrifice to be eaten (and possibly cooked offsite), Leviticus 1:8-9 required that the head, fat, inwards and legs of each large animal be burned on the altar. For birds, Leviticus 1:14-17 required that the entire bird excluding the crop be burned on the altar. Leviticus 1:7 required that the altar have a fire fueled by wood, which could not possibly burn that much animal biomass in less than 1 minute.

At the rate of about one sacrifice a minute, within just a few minutes the altar would have become an overflowed mound of dismembered parts and blood which would snuff out the fire and spill over onto the floor. It is simply not possible that this one altar could perform more than a miniscule fraction of the ritual sacrifices that Old Testament Law required over a million Hebrew men and women to perform.

How Many Cities Were Given To Judah?

Joshua 15:21-32 is unusual even by Biblical standards because it contradicts itself. There are **38** cities listed, but the last verse says, "all the cities are **twenty and nine**".

1- Kabzeel	2 - Eder	3 - Jagur	4 - Kinah
5 - Dimonah	6 - Adadah	7 - Kedesh	8 - Hazor
9 - Ithnan	10 - Ziph	11 - Telem	12 - Bealoth
13 - Hazor	14 - Hadattah	15 - Kerioth	16 - Hezron (Hazor)
17 - Amam	18 - Shema	19 - Moladah	20 - Hazar-gaddah
21 - Heshmon	22 - Beth-palet	23 - Hazar-shual	24 - Beer-sheba
25 - Bizjothjah	26 - Baalah	27 - Iim	28 - Azem
29 - Eltolad	30 - Chesil	31 - Hormah	32 - Ziklag
33 - Madmannah	34 - Sansannah	35 - Lebaoth	36 - Shilhim
37 - Ain	38 - Rimmon		

*   *   *

How Many Cities Were In The Valley?

Joshua 15:33-36 lists **15** cities that were in the valley and were given to the tribe of Judah. But the last verse says that there were, **"fourteen cities"**.

1 - Eshtaol	2 - Zoreah	3 - Ashnah	4 - Zanoah
5 - En-gannim	6 - Tappuah	7 - Enam,	8 - Jarmuth
9 - Adullam	10 - Socoh	11 - Azekah	12 - Sharaim
13 - Adithaim	14 - Gederah	15 - Gederothaim	

How Many Israelite Tribes Were There?

It is generally accepted that there were twelve tribes of Israel. But the Bible contradicts itself when it names the tribes.

Genesis 49:3-28	Exodus 1:1-5	Numbers 13:2-15	Revelation 7:4-8
Reuben	Reuben	Reuben	Reuben
Simeon	Simeon	Simeon	Simeon
Levi	Levi	--	Levi
Judah	Judah	Judah	Judah
Zebulun	Zebulun	Zebulun	Zebulun
Isaachar	Isaachar	Isaachar	Isaachar
Dan	Dan	Dan	--
Gad	Gad	Gad	Gad
Asher	Asher	Asher	Asher
Naphtali	Naphtali	Naphtali	Naphtali
Joseph	Joseph	Joseph	Joseph
Benjamin	Benjamin	Benjamin	Benjamin
		Ephraim	--
			Manasses

According to Genesis 48:5, Ephraim and Manasses were sons of Joseph. Since the Numbers 13:2-15 and Revelation 7:4-8 lists contain both Joseph and one of his sons, these two passages effectively list the tribe of Joseph twice.

* * *

Was Moses Active Or Debilitated When He Was 120 Years Old?

Two passages in the Bible claim that Moses lived to the ripe old age of 120 years. But these passages, just a few chapters apart, contradict each other when describing his physical condition at that age.

Deuteronomy 31:1-2 says, "Moses went and spake these words unto all Israel. And he said unto them, I am an hundred and twenty years old this day. I can no more go out and come in."

But just a few chapters later, Deuteronomy 34:7 says, "Moses was an hundred and twenty years old when he died. His eye was not dim, nor his natural force abated."

How Many Sons Did Jesse have?

Jesse was the father of King David. The book of 1 Samuel says twice that Jesse had eight sons and that David was the youngest. 1 Samuel 16:10-13 says, "Jesse made seven of his sons to pass before Samuel ... And Samuel said unto Jesse, Are here all thy children? And he said, There remaineth yet the youngest ... Samuel said unto Jesse, Send and fetch him ... and he sent, and brought him in ... Then Samuel took the horn of oil, and anointed him in the midst of his brethren, and the Spirit of the Lord came upon David from that day forward". 1 Samuel 17:12-14 says, "David was the son of ... Jesse, and he had **eight sons ... David was the youngest**".

But 1 Chronicles 2:13-15 says that Jesse had only seven sons. "Jesse begat his firstborn Eliab, and Abinadab the second, and Shimma the third, Nethaneel the fourth, Raddai the fifth, Ozem the sixth, **David the seventh**."

*   *   *

How Big Was David's Army?

2 Samuel chapter 24 and 1 Chronicles chapter 21 describe the same events: David took a census and God sent a plague. This bizarre episode is described in detail in "How Do You Prevent A Plague Or Cause One? Take A Census!" on the next page of this book.

Samuel and Chronicles contradict each other when reporting the numerical results of this census. 2 Saumel 24:9 says, "Joab gave up the sum of the number of the people unto the king, and there were in Israel eight hundred thousand valiant men that drew the sword; and the men of Judah were five hundred thousand men". So 2 Samuel claims that they counted 800,000 + 500,000 = 1,300,000 men capable of going to war in Israel and Judah combined.

1 Chronicles 21:5 says "Joab gave the sum of the number of the people unto David. And all they of Israel were a thousand thousand and an hundred thousand men that drew sword, and Judah was four hundred threescore and ten thousand men that drew sword". So 1 Chronicles claims that there were 1,100,000 + 470,000 = 1,570,000 men capable of going to war in Israel and Judah combined.

1 Chronicles 21:6 says that the number in verse 5 actually understated the true number because it omitted two tribes, "But Levi and Benjamin counted he not among them, for the king's word was abominable to Joab". The Bible does not say how large the tribe of Benjamin was at that time, but 2 Chronicles 14:8 says that in the time of King Asa (David's great-great-grandson), Judah and Benjamin were about the same size.

How Do You Prevent A Plague Or Cause One? Take A Census!

Exodus 30:11-12 says, "The Lord spake unto Moses, saying, When thou takest the sum of the children of Israel after their number ... thou numberest them; **that there be no plague** among them, when thou numberest them". Since God had recently sent 10 plagues upon Egypt, this was no idle threat. Obviously, the way to prevent God from sending a plague was to count the Israelites. So they reported in Exodus 38:26 that there were 603,550 adult Israelite men and a plague was averted.

There are many censuses in the Bible. God commanded that the Hebrews conduct a census that is reported in Nehemiah chapter 7 and Ezra chapter 2. Luke 2:1 says that a Roman census was the reason that Jesus was born in Bethlehem. There is an entire book of the Bible called "Numbers". From this you might conclude that God would not mind if someone counted the Hebrews, but you would be mistaken.

2 Samuel 24:1 says, "The anger of the Lord was kindled against Israel, and he moved David against them to say, Go, number Israel and Judah". The Bible doesn't tell us why God was angry, but David did what God "moved" him to do and dutifully counted the all of the Hebrews, about 1,300,000 adult men. You might assume that David's actions, following Moses' example, would have prevented God from sending a plague. But the exact opposite happened.

Somehow, David realized that God was upset, so in 2 Samuel 24:10, "David said unto the Lord, I have sinned greatly in that I have done, and now, I beseech thee, O Lord, take away the iniquity of thy servant, for I have done very foolishly". Since God promises to forgive sins, you might think that after such a nice apology that God would calm down, forgive David, and that would be the end of it. Wrong again.

2 Samuel 24:15 says that God sent a plague that killed 70,000 men in three days. There are several problems with this:
- David did what God "moved" him to do
- Nowhere in the Bible did God tell David not to count Israel and Judah
- Conducting or participating in a census is not a death penalty offense
- God punished the wrong person 70,000 times

David was the one who ordered the census. But God killed 70,000 men, leaving David unharmed. It is difficult to imagine a more arbitrary, capricious and misdirected injustice, committed by a supposedly just and merciful God.

It actually gets worse. 2 Samuel 24:1 says, "the Lord ... moved David" to number Israel. 1 Chronicles 21 reports the same census and plague, but in verse 1 it says, "Satan ... provoked David to number Israel". Sometimes God's behavior is so bad that even the Bible cannot tell the difference between God and Satan!

How Many Years Between Leaving Egypt and Building the Temple?

1 Kings 6:1 says, "It came to pass in the **four hundred and eightieth year** after the children of Israel were come out of the land of Egypt, in the fourth year of Solomon's reign over Israel, in the month Zif, which is the second month, that he began to build the house of the Lord".

But if you do the math, there were substantially more than 480 years between the Israelites leaving Egypt and starting construction on the Temple:

40 years - wandering in the wilderness - Acts 13:18, Deuteronomy 29:5

45 years - conquest of the Holy Land - Joshua 14:7-10

450 years - governed by Judges - Acts 13:20

40 years - reign of King Saul - Acts 13:21

40 years - reign of King David - 2 Samuel 5:4-5, 1 Kings 2:11

4 years - Solomon's reign before Temple construction - 1 Kings 6:1

Total: 40 + 45 + 450 + 40 + 40 + 4 = **619 years**

So 1 Kings 6:1 and the rest of the Bible disagree by 619 - 480 = 169 years.

This discrepancy is actually greater than 169 years because the 450 years reported in Acts 13:20 does not include the judgeship of Samuel:

Name	Reference	Years of Judging
Othniel	Judges 3:8-11	48
Ehud	Judges 3:14, 3:30	98
Shamgar	Judges 3:31	not provided
Deborah/Barak	Judges 4:3, 5:31	60
Gideon	Judges 6:1, 8:28	47
Abimelech	Judges 9:22	3
Tolah	Judges 10:2	23
Jair	Judges 10:3	22
Jephthah	Judges 10:8, 12:7	23
Ibzan	Judges 12:8-10	7
Elon	Judges 12:11-12	10
Abdon	Judges 12:14	8
Samson	Judges 13:1, 15:20, 16:31	60
Eli	1 Samuel 4:18	40
Samuel	1 Samuel 7:15	not provided
	Total:	449 years

This number is close to the number in Acts 13:20, but it does not include the judgeship of Samuel, one of the most famous judges. (In most Bibles, he has two entire books named after him.) Samuel had a very long judgeship lasting from youth to extreme old age. Bible scholars estimate that he judged for 70 years[4].

How Many Tribes Remained Loyal to Solomon's Descendants?

Late in his life, King Solomon committed some sins that greatly offended God. So God told Solomon that he would take away most of his kingdom from his son, leaving only one tribe loyal to his descendants. 1 Kings 11:11-13 says, "I [God] will surely rend the kingdom from thee, and will give it to thy servant. Notwithstanding in thy days I will not do it for David thy father's sake: but I will rend it out of the hand of thy son. Howbeit I will not rend away all the kingdom; but will give **one tribe** to thy son for David my servant's sake."

This claim is repeated in 1 Kings 11:35-36, "I will take the kingdom out of his [Solomon's] son's hand, and will give it unto thee [Jeroboam, who was not related to Solomon], even ten tribes. And unto his son will I give **one tribe**, that David my servant may have a light always before me in Jerusalem, the city which I have chosen me to put my name there". 1 Kings 12:20 makes the same claim, "There was none that followed the house of [Solomon's father] David, but the tribe of Judah only".

But other passages in the Bible say that three tribes, Judah, Benjamin and Levi, stayed loyal to David/Solomon's dynasty. Judah and Benjamin remained under the dominion of Solomon's descendants continually until the deportation to Babylon, according to 1 Kings 12:21 and 12:23, as well as 2 Chronicles 11:1, 11:12, 11:23, 14:8, 15:2, 15:8-9, 25:5, 31:1, 34:9 and 34:32. According to Ezra 1:5 and 4:1, also Nehemiah 11:4 and 11:31-36, the tribes of Judah and Benjamin returned to live in Judea and practice Jehovah worship until the end of Old Testament times.

The Benjamites remained in Judea and kept their tribal identity even in New Testament times, according to Romans 11:1 and Philippians 3:5. Some apologists claim that the tribe of Benjamin was so small that it was irrelevant. But 2 Chronicles 14:8 says that in the time of King Asa (Solomon's great-grandson), Judah and Benjamin were about the same size - Judah had 300,000 soldiers and Benjamin had 280,000 soldiers.

2 Chronicles 11:13-14 says that a third tribe, Levi, also remained loyal to the kings descended from David and Solomon, "The priests and the Levites that were in all Israel resorted to him [Solomon's son Rehoboam] out of all their coasts [Revised Standard Bible says "from all places where they lived"]. For the Levites left their suburbs and their possession, and came to Judah and Jerusalem; for Jeroboam and his sons had cast them off from executing the priest's office unto the Lord".

Levites continued to live in Jerusalem at least until New Testament times, according to John 1:19 and Acts 4:36.

Baasha Fought A Battle 9 Years After He And His Family Died

1 Kings 16:6-8 says, "Baasha [king of Israel] slept with his fathers, and was buried in Tirzah: and Elah his son reigned in his stead ... In the **twenty and sixth** year of Asa king of Judah began Elah the son of Baasha to reign over Israel".

Not only did Baasha die in the 26th year of Asa's reign, every male of Baasha's family was killed in the 27th year of Asa's reign. 1 Kings 16:9-12 says, "His [Elah's] servant Zimri, captain of half his chariots, conspired against him ... Zimri went in and smote him, and killed him, in the **twenty and seventh year** of Asa king of Judah, and reigned in his stead. And it came to pass, when he began to reign, as soon as he sat on his throne, that he slew all the house of Baasha. He left him not one that pisseth against a wall, neither of his kinsfolks, nor of his friends. Thus did Zimri destroy all the house of Baasha". This completely eliminates the possibility that "Baasha" could be interpreted to mean Baasha's dynasty or descendants.

But 2 Chronicles 16:1 says, "In the **six and thirtieth year** of the reign of Asa, Baasha king of Israel came up against Judah". 2 Chronicles 16:2-6, says that Baasha had formed an alliance with the king of Damascus and that he was fortifying the city of Ramah. Not bad for a guy who has been dead for more than 9 years.

* * *

How Many Jews Did Nebuchadrezzar/Nebuchadnezzar Deport?

Jeremiah 52:28-30 gives the number of Jews deported by the Babylonians, "This is the people whom Nebuchadrezzar carried away captive, in the seventh year **three thousand Jews and three and twenty**, in the eighteenth year of Nebuchadrezzar he carried away captive from Jerusalem **eight hundred thirty and two** persons, in the three and twentieth year of Nebuchadrezzar Nebuzaradan the captain of the guard carried away captive of the Jews **seven hundred forty and five** persons, all the persons were four thousand and six hundred". 3023 + 832 + 745 = 4600.

But 2 Kings 24:14 says, "He [Nebuchadnezzar] carried away all Jerusalem, and all the princes, and all the mighty men of valour, even **ten thousand** captives".

Victory Or Defeat? It Depends . . .

2 Chronicles 28:5-8 says, "The Lord his [Judah's king Ahaz] God delivered him into the hand of the king of Syria; and they smote him, and carried away a great multitude of them captives, and brought them to Damascus. And he was also delivered into the hand of the king of Israel, who smote him with a great slaughter. For Pekah the son of Remaliah slew in Judah an **hundred and twenty thousand** in one day, which were all valiant men; because they had forsaken the Lord God of their fathers. Zichri ... slew Maaseiah the king's son, and Azrikam the governor of the house, and Elkanah that was next to the king. And the children of Israel carried away captive of their brethren **two hundred thousand**, women, sons, and daughters, and took also away much spoil from them, and brought the spoil to Samaria."

This is about as bleak a picture of complete defeat as a person can imagine. King Ahaz's army suffered 120,000 soldiers killed in a single day, a great multitude were captured and carried away to Damascus in Syria, and his own son plus two of his closest assistants were killed. In addition, over 200,000 women and children were taken away captive to Israel in Samaria.

But 2 Kings 16:5 tells a very different story. "Rezin king of Syria and Pekah son of Remaliah king of Israel came up to Jerusalem to war, and they besieged Ahaz, but could not overcome him".

* * *

20,000 Divine Chariots vs. 2-Horsepower Wheeled Washtubs

Psalm 68:17 says, "The chariots of God are twenty thousand, even thousands of angels". Although the firepower of a "chariot of God" is not defined, surely one Godly chariot could easily out-fight one modern tank or jet fighter. At present, Israel adequately defends itself against modern enemy armies with less than one-tenth this number of tanks and jets combined. So 20,000 of these supernatural chariots would be an overwhelming force even by twenty-first century standards.

The claim of Psalm 68:17 contradicts Judges 1:19, which says, "And the Lord was with Judah, and He drove out the inhabitants of the mountain, but could not drive out the inhabitants of the valley, because they had chariots of iron". Usually when the armies of Israel had a problem, the Bible says it was due to some kind of sin. Not this time. The Bible makes it clear that "the Lord was with Judah", but that was no help against 2-horsepower wheeled washtubs driven by heathens armed only with arrows, spears and swords.

Once again, we see an evolving myth. Judges 1:19 clearly describes a tribal deity of limited power, who is very different from the almighty deity in Psalm 68.

Two Really Old Brick Layers

In Ezra 1:1-4, Persia's king Cyrus decreed the Israelites exiled in Babylon could, "go up to Jerusalem ... and build the house of the Lord God of Israel". This happened in the first year of Cyrus' reign. Ezra chapters 2-3 say that Cyrus provided large numbers of camels, asses, mules and horses, as well as money, enabling over 42,000 Israelites to quickly return to Jerusalem. Ezra 3:2-8 says that two of their leaders at that time were Zerubbabel son of Shealtiel and Jeshua son of Jozadak.

The Persian kings during the time of the last books of the Old Testament are:

Cyrus	555 - 529 BCE	(Ezra 1:1-8, 3:7, 4:5)
Ahasuerus/Cambyses	529 - 522 BCE	(Ezra 4:6, Daniel 9:1)
Darius I	521 - 485 BCE	(Ezra 4:5)
Xerxes	485 - 464 BCE	
Artaxerxes I	464 - 423 BCE	(Ezra Chapters 4, 7 and 8)
Darius II	423 - 404 BCE	(Ezra 4:24, 5:5-6:15)
Artaxerxes II (Mnemon)	404 - 359 BCE	
Artaxerxes III	359 - 338 BCE	

In Ezra chapter 4, enemies of the Israelites persuaded Artaxerxes to order the Israelites to stop building the temple. Verses 23-24 say, "When the copy of king Artaxerxes' letter was read ... Then ceased the work of the house of God which is at Jerusalem. So it ceased unto the second year of the reign of Darius king of Persia". This had to be Darius II, because it happened after the reign of Artaxerxes, who had ordered the construction to stop.

Just two verses later, Ezra 5:2 says, "Zerubbabel son of Shealtiel and Jeshua the son of Jozadak ... began to build the house of God which is at Jerusalem". Ezra 5:6-8 says three times that this happened during the reign of Darius, who gave them permission for them to continue building the temple in Ezra 6:7-14. The temple was finished in the sixth year of Darius' reign, according to Ezra 6:15.

The problem is that Zerubbabel son of Shealtiel and Jeshua son of Jozadak were already adults in the first year of Cyrus, 555 BCE, old enough to lead the Hebrews on a long journey from Persia to Jerusalem. But Ezra 5:2-7 says they were working on the temple again in the second year of Darius II, i.e., 422 BCE. Zechariah 4:9 also claims that Zerubbabel started and finished the temple.

If Zerubbabel and Jeshua were at least 20 years old in 555 BCE (Ezra 3:8), then they would have been at least 153 years old in 422 BCE. It is difficult to imagine them being alive, much less doing manual labor or supervising a large construction project, at that age. Although early books of the Bible do claim that some people lived very long lives, the Bible does not claim that anyone after the time of the Judges lived to be over 100 years old.

How Many Vessels Did Cyrus Give To The Temple?

Ezra 1:7-11 says that Persia's king, "Cyrus ... brought forth the vessels [Hebrew "keli"] of the house of the Lord" and sent them back to Jerusalem for God's temple. Ezra 1:9-10 gives an itemized inventory, "And this is the number of them":

30	chargers of gold
1000	chargers of silver
29	knives
30	basons of gold
410	silver basons of a second sort
1000	other vessels [keli]

Then Ezra 1:11 sums it up for us, "All the vessels [keli] of gold and of silver were five thousand and four hundred. All these did Sheshbazzar bring up with them of the captivity that were brought up from Babylon unto Jerusalem".

The problem is that 30 + 1000 + 29 + 30 + 410 + 1000 = 2,499, not 5,400. Interestingly, this self-contradiction was one of the first to be recognized by Bible scholars. Some ancient manuscripts[5] have comments written in their margins indicating that scribes had noticed that these numbers did not add up.

*   *   *

Bad Accounting

The Bible says that many Hebrews made contributions towards the rebuilding of the Jerusalem Temple, but Ezra and Nehemiah disagree on the amounts.

Ezra 2:68-69 says, "Some of the chief of the fathers, when they came to the house of the Lord which is at Jerusalem, offered freely for the house of God to set it up in his place. They gave after their ability unto the treasure of the work threescore and one thousand drams of gold, and five thousand pound of silver, and one hundred priests' garments".

Nehemiah 7:70-71 says, "Some of the chief of the fathers gave unto the work. The Tirshatha gave to the treasure a thousand drams of gold, fifty basons, five hundred and thirty priests' garments. And some of the chief of the fathers gave to the treasure of the work twenty thousand drams of gold, and two thousand and two hundred pound of silver".

Items	Ezra's amount	Nehemiah's amount	Difference
Gold (drams)	61,000	1000 + 20,000 = 21,000	40,000
Silver (pounds)	5,000	2,200	2,800
Priest garments	100	530	430

How Many Jews Returned from The Babylonian Captivity?

Ezra chapter 2 provides a census, by family, of people who returned from the Babylonian captivity. Nehemiah chapter 7 provides a census of the same people who returned from the same captivity. Some of these numbers match, proving that it was the same census; others do not, proving that the Bible contradicts itself.

Family	# in Ezra [chapter : verse]		# in Nehemiah [chapter : verse]		Difference
Parosh	2172	[2:3]	2172	[7:8]	0
Shephathiah	372	[2:4]	372	[7:9]	0
Arah	775	[2:5]	652	[7:10]	123
Pahathmoab, Jeshua & Joab	2812	[2:6]	2818	[7:11]	6
Elam	1254	[2:7]	1254	[7:12]	0
Zattu	945	[2:8]	845	[7:13]	100
Zaccai	760	[2:9]	760	[7:14]	0
Bani (Bennui)	642	[2:10]	648	[7:15]	6
Bebai	623	[2:11]	628	[7:16]	5
Azgad	1222	[2:12]	2322	[7:17]	1100
Adonikam	666	[2:13]	667	[7:18]	1
Bigvai	2056	[2:14]	2067	[7:19]	11
Adin	454	[2:15]	655	[7:20]	201
Ater	98	[2:16]	98	[7:21]	0
Bezai	323	[2:17]	324	[7:23]	1
Jorah	112	[2:18]	missing		112
Hashum	223	[2:19]	328	[7:22]	105
Gibbar (Gibeon)	95	[2:20]	95	[7:25]	0
Bethlehem & Netophah	179	[2:21-22]	188	[7:26]	9
Anathoth	128	[2:23]	128	[7:27]	0
Azamveth	42	[2:24]	42	[7:28]	0
Kirjath-arim, Chephirah & Beeroth	743	[2:25]	743	[7:29]	0
Ramah, Gabah	621	[2:26]	621	[7:30]	0
Lod, Hadid & Ono	725	[2:33]	721	[7:37]	4
Senaah	3630	[2:35]	3930	[7:38]	300
Asaph	128	[2:41]	148	[7:44]	20
Shallum, Ater, Talmon, Akkub, Hatita & Shoba	139	[2:42]	138	[7:45]	1
Delaiah, Tobiah & Nekoda	652	[2:60]	642	[7:62]	10
Total Difference:					**2117**

Note: Some families have been omitted to save space. The Ezra and Nehemiah counts match each other for all families that I omitted from this list.

Chapter 4

Sexual Math Mistakes

The Bible is never more dogmatic, irrational, self-contradictory and hypo-critical than when it attempts to regulate sexual behavior. God mandated fidelity yet commanded Hosea to marry a whore. God prohibited marriage to Pagans, yet Esther did so and saved the entire Hebrew nation from annihilation. Jesus figured out a way to make wives guilty of adultery even if they were completely faithful to their husbands - an unavoidable sin!

This duplicitous morality has resulted in confused sexual behavior. Throughout most of its history, the Church tried to pretend that sex did not exist, except rarely and grudgingly for the purpose of procreating new Christians. This led to widespread pedophilia and other sexual abuses committed by priests, ministers and lay church leaders. Sexual abuses by church leaders, and the deceitful and cruel coverups, are traditions that are almost as old and pervasive as communion[1]. These abuses are only being revealed now because the church has lost the power to silence its victims.

One of the great social changes of the twentieth century is the widespread acknowledgement that sex is actually fun. At the same time, Christendom has lost much of its power to control sexual behavior in civil law and even among its own believers. This has resulted in some of the greatest doctrinal shifts in the history of Christianity. Clear Bible commands that have been accepted as infallibly true for almost 2,000 years have been discarded as gleefully as participants in an orgy shed their underwear.

Divorce used to be a sin because Jesus said it was in Matthew 19:4-8. Jesus specifically condemned marrying a divorcee in Matthew 19:9 and Mark 10:11-12. But modern conservative Christians have some of the highest divorce rates and many churches have "single again" ministries designed to help divorced Christians re-marry.

Christians used to regard pregnancy outside of marriage as shameful to the entire family and would hide the new mother or send her to live somewhere else as soon as her waistline began to expand. If the girl was a minister's daughter, it invariably ended his career because 1 Timothy 3:4-5 says that a church leader must, "Rule well his own house, having his children in subjection with all gravity. For if a man know not how to rule his own house, how shall he take care of the church of God?" Nowadays, anti-abortionists hail unmarried teenage mothers as heroes, while at the same time proclaiming the effectiveness of abstinence-only sex education.

It is just about impossible to think about math at the same time you are thinking about sex. Who would want to? Apparently the Bible's authors had the same difficulty, because the Bible contains numerous sexy math mistakes, many of which call into question some of Christianity's most widespread and dogmatic beliefs.

Most Prolific Human Procreation In History

Exodus 6:14-25 contains the genealogies of some important Israelites during the years that the Hebrews were in Egypt. Note that there are only four generations listed (see below). This genealogy is repeated in 1 Chronicles chapters 6 and 23. These assertions that the Israelites spent only four generations in Egypt are corroborated by Genesis 15:16, where God told Abraham, "In the fourth generation they shall come hither again".

As documented in "Were The Israelites In Egypt 255, 350 or 430 years?" in Chapter 3, the Bible makes several self-contradictory statements about the number of years the Israelites spent in Egypt. But it is quite consistent about the number of generations: **exactly 4**. If there were more than 4 generations, God's prophecy to Abraham in Genesis 15:16 would be false. The Bible attempts to make this plausible by claiming that the Hebrews had very long lifespans during this time.

The Bible also claims that the Israelites experienced an enormous population explosion while they were in Egypt - growing from 70-75 males according to Exodus 1:5, to about 600,000 adult males according to Exodus 12:37 and Numbers 1:46. To accomplish this, each generation would have to experience a twenty-fold increase in the number of males:

Generation #1 (at the time of Levi)	75 males
Generation #2 (at the time of Kohath)	75 * 20 = 1500 males
Generation #3 (at the time of Amram)	1500 * 20 = 30,000 males
Generation #4 (when Moses was 80)	30,000 * 20 = 600,000 males

Since about half of humans are born female, each Israelite woman would have to have given birth, on average, to 40 children who survived to adulthood, and all of each woman's 20 female children would have had to have given birth to an average of 40 babies who survived to adulthood, for 4 consecutive generations.

This claim of extreme growth is supported by Numbers 3:40-43, "The Lord said unto Moses, Number all the firstborn of the males of the children of Israel from a month old and upward ... all the firstborn males ... from a month old and upward ... were twenty and two thousand two hundred and threescore and thirteen [22,273]". Since Numbers 1:46 says that there were 603,550 adult males at about this same time, each "firstborn male" would have had over two dozen brothers.

Nothing remotely approaching this has ever been achieved in any human population in history.

Then, mysteriously, this population explosion came to a screeching halt.. Numbers 26:51 says that their population actually dropped to 601,730 adult males by the end of their 40 years in the wilderness. So did their abnormally long lifespans, because Numbers 32:11-13 says that all but 2 of them died during those 40 years.

Profuse, Open, Sexual Sin Every Day While Writing the Bible

Arguably the holiest thing that any follower of God could do would be to write part of the Bible. We are not told how many individuals belong to the elite group of Bible Authors. But we can be certain that it is very small and that it **ex**cludes some of the greatest theologians in history, such as Augustine, Aquinas, Luther, Wesley and Hillel.

Tens of millions of Christian conservatives believe that the Bible is a perfect book, completely without error in the original manuscripts[2]. Just imagine how obedient to God a person would have to be to write anything that is word-for-word so divine that it does not have even the possibility of having the slightest error!

So you would expect that 100% of the writers of the Bible would know when to keep their pants on. Most of them did, we are told. But the Bible says that there are two notable exceptions: David, who wrote many Psalms, and Solomon, who wrote most (or all) of Proverbs, Song of Solomon and Ecclesiastes.

The Bible tolerates polygamy in many cases. The New Testament prohibits it only for church leaders. Old Testament Law permitted polygamy for most Hebrews. Some Bible believers argue that this was a compassionate thing to do. For example, if a man died, his widow could marry her husband's brother even if he was already married.

Polygamy was **not** permitted for all Hebrews, however. Old Testament Law very clearly prohibited Hebrew kings from having more than one wife. Deuteronomy 17:17 commands that a Hebrew king, "Neither shall he multiply wives to himself".

King David enthusiastically violated this Law of God. 2 Samuel 3:2-5 names sons that David fathered by six of his wives. Add Bathsheba (2 Samuel 12:24), and you get 7 wives who had children by David. Many apologists argue that ancient polygamy was more of a political and economic contract than a sexual relationship, so polygamous marriages were often not consummated sexually and did not violate the objections that most modern people have against polygamy. These verses disprove that argument because they clearly say that David fathered children by these wives.

David's polygamy pales beside that of his son Solomon, who "had seven hundred wives, princesses and three hundred concubines," according to 1 Kings 11:3. Solomon could literally have had sex with a different wife every day for almost 2 years without banging the same one twice.

David and Solomon's polygamy was quite open. It was continuous - lasting their entire adult lives. Their priests, subjects and biographers knew about it. It was very clear that God's own Law prohibited it. But they wrote major parts of the Bible anyway, perfectly inspired by God while living in constant, open, sexual sin.

The Bible Says That Women Are Worth Less Than Men

One of the most basic principles of all modern democracies and republics is that all human beings are of equal value. This is codified into numerous laws which require that women vote on an equal basis with men, be paid the same wages for the same work, have the same employment opportunities, etc.

This equality is absent from the Bible. For example, Leviticus 27:2 says, "When a man shall make a singular vow, the persons shall be for the Lord by thy estimation". What follows in verses 3-7 is an explicit quantification of the fact that the Bible places a lower value on women than men, in shekels of silver:

	Male	Female
20-60 years old	50	30
5-20 years old	20	10
1 month - 5 years	5	3
Over 60 years old	15	10

The writers of the New Testament nullified the Old Testament requirements for paying money to Jewish priests. (Not coincidentally, none of them were Jewish priests.) So these bargain basement prices for women do not apply to Christians.

But many conservative churches, and the entire Catholic church, continue to deny their highest paying jobs to women because they do not allow them to be ministers or priests. This is based on New Testament passages such as 1 Timothy 2:11-15 and 1 Corinthians 14:34-35.

These churches and denominations are absolutely convinced that Jesus has told them to never let a woman be minister or priest. But many other churches and denominations are equally sincere and equally convinced that Jesus has told them the exact opposite - that Jesus actively recruits women to be ministers or priests. Many denominations on opposite sides of this issue are equally conservative: Southern Baptists prohibit women from preaching, Pentecostals encourage it. Why is Jesus telling some Christians one thing and telling the exact opposite to other Christians?

As previously noted, changes in society's attitudes towards sex have caused the church to abandon doctrines which it used to preach as absolute, eternal truth. These changes are powerful evidence in favor of a dirty little secret about church dogma: it is driven by marketing, not revelation, and is as malleable as it needs to be to maximize attendance and contributions.

I therefore make the following prophecy. Thus sayeth Robert: The modern church is having great difficulty recruiting enough ministers and priests. When job applicants get so scarce that the existence of a denomination is threatened by a lack of priests or ministers, God will miraculously reveal to denominational leaders that he now wants women to fill jobs that he used to tell them were off-limits.

"1 Flesh" Can Get Very Kinky

Genesis 2:24 says, "Therefore shall a man leave his father and his mother, and shall cleave [cling] unto his wife and they shall be one flesh". This idea is repeated in 1 Corinthians 6:16, "Know ye not that he which is joined to an harlot is one body? For two, saith he, shall be one flesh".

Christians apply these verses to a wide range of (preferentially enforced) sexual taboos related to marital fidelity and abstinence outside of marriage. Based on these verses, Christians believe that you become "one flesh" with everyone you have sex with. The Bible does not give us any more detail about what it means to be "one flesh" with someone, but God's followers assure us that it will cause you to have terrible psychological problems if you spread your "one flesh" to more than one person or to a person of the wrong gender.

Convincing evidence against this belief comes from ministers and other professional Christians who secretly spread their "flesh" widely among women, and sometimes other men and/or even children[1], yet continue preaching sermons on Sundays, sermons which their congregations continue to believe are filled with the power of the Holy Spirit. If these are such bad sins, why don't the people in the pews notice that the Power of God is no longer with their minister? The fact is that many paid Christians commit fornication, adultery and even molestation for years, while their followers continue to believe that God speaks through these ministers who secretly practice what they condemn from their pulpits. The followers also continue to believe that God has told them to pay these hypocrites as though they were still doing his will. Why can they get away with this so often? The only reasonable explanation is that it is just too easy to fake it, particularly when money is involved.

Other Bible passages reveal more problems with the "one flesh" claim, because many of the Bible's most respected role models were polygamous.

Jacob/Israel fathered children by two wives and two "maids". Gideon, the inspiration for the Bible in your hotel room, had "many wives". Abraham fathered a son with Hagar, his wife's "maidservant", and also by his wife Sarah. David fathered children by seven wives; Solomon had 700 wives and 300 concubines. So Solomon became "one flesh" with wife #1, then he became "one flesh" with wife #2. Since Solomon was already "one flesh" with wife #1, did that automatically make wife #2 "one flesh" with wife #1? What about wives #699 and #700, and all the others in between? Was David 1/7 of one flesh with each of his wives?

The "one flesh" idea is a nice thought for monogamous relationships, but for Biblical role models like David, Gideon, Abraham, Jacob and Solomon, it got pretty kinky.

Benjamin - the Child Who Was A Grandfather

Benjamin and Joseph were the two youngest sons of Jacob/Israel and the only sons of his favorite wife, Rachel. Joseph is the main character of the last dozen chapters of Genesis. According to Genesis 37:2-3, "Israel loved Joseph more than all his children, because he was the son of his old age". Joseph's brothers sold him to slave traders and convinced Israel that he had been killed by wild animals. After travails and miracles, Genesis 41:43 says that Pharaoh appointed Joseph, "ruler over all the land of Egypt".

Rachel died giving birth to Benjamin, who must have been born after Israel believed Joseph was dead. Otherwise Ben, not Joseph, would have been "the son of Israel's old age". Later, Ben became the "child of [Israel's] old age" in Genesis 44:20.

Genesis 46:21 says that Benjamin had ten sons when Israel's extended family moved to Egypt to live with Joseph and escape a famine, "The sons of Benjamin were Belah, Becher, Ashbel, Gera, Naaman, Ehi, Rosh, Muppim, Huppim and Ard". According to Numbers 26:38-40, Naaman and Ard were actually Benjamin's grandsons.

Genesis chapter 46 cannot be interpreted as saying that Bejnamin fathered these sons and/or grandsons after going to Egypt, because it lists the names of every one of Israel's direct descendants living at the time of the trip, including even one daughter. It excludes Benjamin's two nephews who had died, Er and Onan. This chapter identifies the only two descendants of Israel who were born in Egypt: Joseph's two sons. It then gives a count of the named individuals, "all the souls of the house of Jacob, which came into Egypt, were threescore and ten [seventy]" in verse 27 (see also Exodus 1:5). Without Benjamin's sons, there would only be sixty.

Genesis says that Benjamin was quite young at the time he, his sons and grandsons migrated to Egypt. A year or less before he entered Egypt, he was called a "child" and a "little one" in Genesis 44:20 and a "lad" six times in Genesis 44:22-34.

We can calculate a maximum age for Benjamin at the time he entered Egypt. According to Genesis 37:2, Joseph was 17 when he went to Egypt. Genesis 41:46 says that Joseph was 30 when Pharaoh put him in power. Then there were 7 years of plentiful harvest, followed by a famine. According to Genesis 45:6-11, Israel and his family moved to Egypt in the 2nd or 3rd year of the famine.

$$(30-17) + 7 + 3 = 23 \text{ years old}$$

This maximum age is a bit too old for the Bible's statements that Benjamin was a "lad" and a "child". Maybe he was younger, or maybe 23 was younger than it appears, because Benjamin's father Israel lived 147 years and his brother Levi lived to be 137. If he really was a "child", "little one" or "lad", it raises the obvious question of how he could have fathered 10 sons. Whether he was a young adult or a much younger "child" and "lad", it is absurd to claim that he had 2 grandsons.

Inescapable Adulteries > Zero

One of Christianity's most important beliefs is that you do not have to sin if you don't want to. Many Bible passages support this belief. Matthew 6:13 says, "Lead us not into temptation, but deliver us from evil". 1 Corinthians 10:13, says, "God ... will not suffer [allow] you to be tempted above that ye are able; but will with the temptation also make a way to escape, that ye may be able to bear it".

If these verses were true, then we would expect that there would be **zero** situations in which believers would have no control over whether they committed a particular sin. God would be unjust, arbitrary, capricious and cruel if he punished you for a sin that was inescapable.

The Bible actually contains many inescapable sins, i.e., situations in which God's followers had no choice but to do something that was very strongly prohibited by God himself. Some of these are described in "Inescapable Sins > 0" in Chapter 5.

Adultery is a very serious sin according to the Bible. It is forbidden by the Ten Commandments (Exodus 20 and Deuteronomy 5 versions), and was a death penalty offense in Deuteronomy 22:22. Although the New Testament does not punish adultery as harshly, it still regards adultery as one of the most serious sins.

So it may come as a surprise that Jesus himself made adultery an inescapable sin for some people. In Matthew 5:32, Jesus said, "whosoever shall put away his wife, saving for the cause of fornication, causeth her to commit adultery". It is difficult to imagine a more unfair statement: a man can cause a woman to commit adultery without the woman doing anything wrong.

If Jesus was correct, even if a woman was a virgin when she married, was 100% faithful in marriage and did not want the divorce, she will become an adulteress the moment her husband divorces her, making her violate Exodus 20:14, Deuteronomy 5:18, Matthew 19:18, Mark 10:19 and Luke 18:20.

To make matters worse, Jesus established different standards for women and men. If a man divorces his wife, Jesus said that he makes her an adulteress, but Jesus did not say that the man becomes an adulterer. Nor did Jesus say that a man becomes an adulterer if his wife divorces him.

It gets even worse. Jesus went on to say, "whosoever shall marry her that is divorced committeth adultery" in Matthew 5:32. So a woman who became divorced through no fault of her own was deprived of all future opportunities to have a loving husband. This was particularly unfair in ancient male-dominated societies where women had few job opportunities.

Now that Christians have some of the highest divorce rates, however, this draconian command of Jesus is enthusiastically ignored and just about all church leaders encourage divorced Christians to re-marry other divorced Christians.

How Many Sons Did Abraham Have?

The book of Galatians repeatedly claims to have been written by the Apostle Paul. It proclaims just as confidently that Paul got his information straight from God.

The Bible says that Paul had received a Bible-based education that was one of the best available in the Jewish world at that time. Acts 22:3 claims that Paul was, "brought up ... at the feet of Gamaliel, and taught according to the perfect manner of the law of the fathers". Acts 5:34-40 reports that Gamaliel was a member of the ruling council of the Jews in Jerusalem and that he had a very highly regarded, "reputation among all the people", a reputation that was so great that he could sway the decision of the entire council.

Despite claims of Bible expertise and Divine inspiration, the author of Galatians was wrong about something very important in the life of Abraham, one of the most important people in Jewish history and theology.

Galatians 4:22 says, "For it is written, that Abraham had **two sons,** the one by a bondmaid, the other by a freewoman". According to Genesis 16:1-6, Abraham's first son, Ishmael, was the son of his wife's slave Hagar.

Abraham's second son, Isaac, was the son of his wife Sarah, according to Genesis 21:1-5. Sarah was a "freewoman", or at least as free as a woman could be in that culture.

The Bible says very clearly that Abraham fathered many more sons after Ishmael and Isaac. Genesis 25:1-2 says that after Sarah died,

> "Then again Abraham took a wife, and her name was Keturah. And she bare him Zimran, and Jokshan, and Medan, and Midian, and Ishbak, and Shuah. And Jokshan begat Sheba, and Dedan. And the sons of Dedan were Asshurim, and Letushim, and Leummim. And the sons of Midian; Ephah, and Epher, and Hanoch, and Abida, and Eldaah. All these were the children of Keturah."

Not only does Genesis say that Abraham had many more sons, it says that those sons had many children of their own.

It is certain that these were sons because 1 Chronicles 1:32 says, "Now the **sons** of Keturah, Abraham's concubine: she bare Zimran, and Jokshan, and Medan, and Midian, and Ishbak, and Shuah". (Note also that Genesis contradicts Chronicles because Genesis says that Keturah was his "wife" [Hebrew "ishshah"], but Chronicles says that she was his "concubine" [Hebrew "pilegesh"].)

Galatians 4:22 is wrong when it says that Abraham had only 2 sons. The Bible says that Abraham had **8 sons** and even gives us their names.

Chapter 5

Theological Math Mistakes

Mathematical analysis provides a means to evaluate the truth of many of the Bible's theological claims when no other evidence is available. Although the Bible says that all of its claims should be accepted by faith, faith is particularly important for theological statements because these statements are even less verifiable than the Bible's other claims. Archaeologists can provide evidence to support or discredit the Bible's historical claims. But the existence of Heaven is not subject to scientific analysis, so belief in Eternal Life must be accepted entirely on faith. (The converse is not true. It does not take faith to not believe in Heaven, for exactly the same reasons that it does not take faith to not believe in the Valhalla, Nirvana, the Elysian Fields or Pluto's Underworld. There is simply no evidence for any of them.)

As stated in the introduction to this book, we humans constantly make decisions about who and what we can trust. We literally could not live without making these decisions. We have to decide whether the food and water we consume are safe or hazardous. None of us has the equipment or time to evaluate everything we eat or drink for every possible risk. So we make our decisions based on subsets of the evidence, which we can evaluate. We talk to our friends about food safety, read Health Department ratings of restaurants and read published accounts about the safety of our local water supplies. If we hear that a processor of foods or beverages has made a serious error or misled the public about an important safety violation, we can try to get our food and drink elsewhere.

We do this because someone who has misled us about something we know is more likely to mislead us about something we don't know, compared to someone whose statements have been consistently reliable. A product that does not perform as advertised in some of its known characteristics is more likely to have other characteristics that do not perform as advertised.

This simple, common sense approach is particularly effective with the Bible, since it claims to be a perfect book. Disprove any one of the Bible's statements, and an honest person can no longer unquestioningly accept every word of the Bible by faith. The believer will have to make a decision about what parts to believe and not to believe. In short, the believer will have to treat the Bible like any other book.

Some of the most damaging mathematical errors in the Bible are purely theological in nature. Although a single math error of any kind disproves the theological doctrine that the Bible does not contain any errors, some also strike at the very heart of other, very specific, cherished Christian beliefs.

Which Ten Commandments Are The "Real" Ones?

Many Christians are unaware that there is more than one version of the Ten Commandments in the Bible. There are at least three. The first two versions are in Exodus chapter 20 and, with minor variations, Deuteronomy chapter 5:

1. No gods before Jehovah, also known as "The Lord" or "Yahweh"
2. No graven images
3. Do not take The Lord's name in vain
4. Keep the Sabbath
5. Honor your father and mother
6. Do not kill
7. Do not commit adultery
8. Do not steal
9. Do not bear false witness
10. Do not covet

Exodus 32:19 says that Moses broke the stone tablets containing those commandments. So God summoned him back to the mountain, according to Exodus 34:1, "The Lord said unto Moses, 'Hew thee two tables of stone like unto the first: and I will write upon these tables the words that were in the first tables, which thou brakest'".

Much of the rest of Exodus chapter 34 contradicts Exodus 34:1, as well as Exodus chapter 20 and Deuteronomy chapter 5. First of all, Exodus 34:27-28 says that Moses, not God, wrote the Ten Commandments on the stone tables. More importantly, the second Ten Commandments are **not** "the words that were in the first tables". They are very different from the first ones:

1. No covenants with pagan tribes, Exodus 34:12
2. No other gods, Exodus 34:14
3. No molten gods, Exodus 34:17
4. Keep the Feast of Unleavened Bread, Exodus 34:18
5. Every first born animal or human is God's, Exodus 34:19-20
6. Keep the sabbath, Exodus 34:21
7. Observe the Feast of Weeks, Exodus 34:22
8. All male children to appear before God 3 times a year, Exodus 34:23
9. Offer firstfruits of the harvest to God without leaven, Exodus 34:25-26
10. Do not boil a baby goat in its mother's milk, Exodus 34:26

Exodus 34:28 makes it clear that these were in fact the Ten Commandments, "He wrote upon the tables the words of the covenant, the Ten Commandments".

So which Commandments are the real Ten Commandments? According to 1 Kings 8:9 and 2 Chronicles 5:10, the Exodus chapter 34 commandments were the ones that were kept in the Ark of the Covenant, so they were the "official" ones

Inescapable Sins > Zero

"Sin" is one of the most important concepts taught by Christianity. Although Jesus died to forgive Christians' sins, they still have to do everything possible to avoid sinning while they are here on earth. God has promised that he will always enable Christians to avoid sinning. The famous Lord's Prayer in Matthew chapter 6 asks, "Lead us not into temptation, but deliver us from evil". 1 Corinthians 10:13 promises, "God ... will not suffer [allow] you to be tempted above that ye are able; but will with the temptation also make a way to escape, that ye may be able to bear it". (See also James 1:14, Hebrews 4:15, 2 Thessalonians 3:3 and 2 Peter 2:9.)

1 Corinthians 10:13 is about as clear a statement as human language can make, stating conclusively that 100% of sins are avoidable. This is just common sense - it would be unjust for God to punish you for a sin for which you did not have "a way of escape". Unfortunately, the Bible states that has God set people up quite often in ways that make sinning inescapable.

• God commanded "Thou shalt not murder" in Exodus 20:13 and Deuteronomy 5:17. Then he commanded the Hebrews to commit genocide in Deuteronomy 7:1-2 and 20:16-17, orders which were ruthlessly carried out in Joshua chapters 10-11.

• Jesus made some forms of adultery unavoidable. See "Inescapable Adulteries > 0" on page 79 of this book.

• Cannibalism is a sin. But God threatened to make the Jews eat their own children in Jeremiah 19:9, and made good on his threat in Lamentations 2:20 and 4:10.

• God ordered one of the "host of heaven" to commit the sin of lying in 1 Kings 22:20-23 and 2 Chronicles 18:18-22

• 2 Thessalonians 2:10-11 says, "God shall send them strong delusion, that they should believe a lie, that they all might be damned"

• God "moved" David to sin in 2 Samuel chapter 24. Then God killed 70,000 people because David did what God moved him to do. See "How Do You Prevent A Plague Or Cause One? Take A Census!" on page 65 of this book.

• God commanded his followers to swear in Deuteronomy 6:13 and 10:20. But James 5:7-12 and Matthew 5:33-37 condemn swearing

• Romans 13:1-7 and Proverbs 24:21 say that God puts rulers in power and command his followers to obey them. But 1 Kings 14:16 says that king, "Jeroboam ... made Israel to sin". 2 Chronicles 21:9-11 says that king, "Jehoram ... caused the inhabitants of Jerusalem to commit fornication, and compelled Judah thereto"

• 1 John 4:18 says, "There is no fear in love; but perfect love casteth out fear, because fear hath torment. He that feareth is not made perfect in love". Matthew 22:37 commands Christians to love God. But 1 Peter 2:17 and Revelation 14:7 both command Christians to, "Fear God".

How Many Times Do You Get To Die?

Hebrews 9:27 says, "it is appointed to men once to die". The Greek word translated "once" is "hapax", which really does mean "once", i.e., "one time". It is used in 2 Corinthians 11:25, "Thrice was I beaten with rods, once [hapax] was I stoned, thrice I suffered shipwreck", and 1 Peter 3:18, "Christ also hath once [hapax] suffered for sins".

Hebrews 9:27 is surrounded by verses in which "hapax" also very clearly means "one time". Hebrews 9:26 says, "Now once [hapax] in the end of the world hath he [Christ] appeared to put away sin by the sacrifice of himself". Hebrews 9:28 says, "Christ was once [hapax] offered to bear the sins of many". The author of Hebrews used "hapax" three times in a row, each usage unambiguously meaning "one time", in a deliberate literary parallel:

• Christ sacrificed himself once (Hebrews 9:26)
• Men die once (Hebrews 9:27)
• Christ bore the sins of many once (Hebrews 9:28)

Other verses in Hebrews are equally clear that "hapax" means "one time". Hebrews 9:7 says, "Into the second [the Holy of Holies] went the high priest alone once [hapax] every year". Hebrews 12:26-27 says, "Yet once [hapax] more I [God] shake not the earth only, but also heaven, And this word, Yet once [hapax] more, signifieth the removing of those things that are shaken, as of things that are made, that those things which cannot be shaken may remain".

Very clearly, therefore, Hebrews 9:27 says that every human dies precisely one time. This obvious fact is contradicted, however, by other Bible passages.

Genesis 5:23-24 and Hebrews 11:5 say that Enoch did not die because he was taken up directly into Heaven without dying; 2 Kings 2:11 makes the same claim about Elijah. 1 Thessalonians 4:17 says that large numbers of Christians will never die, not even once, because they will be taken directly to Heaven when Jesus returns.

The Bible also says that many people died twice. They died once, then someone raised them from the dead, then they lived for a while and died a second time. Examples include:

• 2 Kings 4:18-37 - The son of a Shunammite woman
• Matthew 27:52-53 - Many "saints which slept" in graves
• Luke 7:11-15 - A dead man in Nain
• John 11:43-44 - Lazarus
• Acts 9:36-41 - Tabitha
• Acts 20:9-12 - Eutychus

How Many Righteous People Have Ever Lived?

Conservative Christian are very clear in their beliefs about human righteousness: there isn't any. Except for Jesus, zero humans have ever been "righteous" or "just". This is essential to the Christian belief that everyone needs to ask Jesus to forgive their sins. If this is not true, Jesus and Christianity are completely unnecessary.

A deeper look at the Bible, however, reveals many contradictions in the basis for this belief. Romans 3:10 says, "There is none righteous, no, not one". The Greek word translated "righteous" in this verse is "dikaios". But Luke 1:5-6 names two righteous people, "There was in the days of Herod ... a certain priest named Zacharias ... his wife ... Elisabeth. And they were both righteous [dikaios] before God". Jesus named two more righteous people in Matthew 23:35, "Upon you may come all the righteous [dikaios] blood shed upon the earth, from the blood of righteous [dikaios] Abel unto the blood of Zacharias son of Barachias".

In Matthew 13:17, Jesus said that there had been "many" righteous people, "Verily I say unto you, that many prophets and righteous [dikaios] men have desired to see those things which ye see". In Matthew 23:29, Jesus said that many people living at that time knew where some of these righteous men were buried, because they, "garnish the sepulchres of the righteous [dikaios]".

The Bible is equally contradictory about whether anyone has ever been "just". Ecclesiastes 7:20 says, "There is not a just man upon earth". The Hebrew word translated "just" in this verse is "tsaddiq". Genesis 6:9 says, "Noah was a just [tsaddiq] man".

In Psalm 18:20-24, king David wrote, "The Lord rewarded me according to my righteousness; according to the cleanness of my hands hath he recompensed me ... Therefore hath the Lord recompensed me according to my righteousness, according to the cleanness of my hands in his eyesight". The Hebrew word translated "righteousness" in these verses is "tsedaqah". If Psalm 18:20-24 is true, David is burning in Hell right now, because Ezekiel 33:12-13 says, "The righteousness [tsedaqah] of the righteous [tsaddiq] shall not deliver him in the day of his transgression ... neither shall the righteous [tsaddiq] be able to live for his righteousness [tsedaqah] in the day that he sinneth. When I [God] say to the righteous [tsaddiq], that he shall surely live, if he trust to his own righteousness [tsedaqah], and commit iniquity, all his righteousnesses [tsedaqah] shall not be remembered, but for his iniquity that he hath committed, he shall die for it."

2 Peter 2:7-8 says that God, "delivered just [dikaios] Lot ... for that righteous [dikaios] man dwelling among them, in seeing and hearing, vexed his righteous [dikaios] soul from day to day with their unlawful deeds". During that same time, Lot offered to let a mob gang rape his two virgin daughters (Genesis 19:4-8).

God Punished The Wrong People, Hundreds Of Years Late

1 Samuel 15:2-3 says that God commanded King Saul, "Thus saith the Lord ... I remember that which Amalek did to Israel, how he laid wait for him in the way, when he came up from Egypt. Now go and smite Amalek, and utterly destroy all that they have, and spare them not; but slay both man and woman, infant and suckling."

God said that he was punishing the Amalekites because of something that had happened over 400 years earlier, shortly after the Hebrews left Egypt, in Exodus 17:8, "Then came Amalek, and fought with Israel in Rephidim". Although the Hebrews won the battle, God was still upset and stated that he would eventually, "utterly put out the remembrance of Amalek from under heaven", in Exodus 17:14.

The obvious problem with God's rationale for the carnage that he commanded in 1 Samuel 15:2-3 is that every one of the Amalekites who had offended him in Exodus 17 had been dead for centuries. Telling King Saul to kill all of the Amalekites because of something that happened during Moses' lifetime would be like telling someone to kill you because King James I, the 17th century English king for whom the King James Bible is named, did not like some of your ancestors.

1 Samuel 15:7-9 says that Saul carried out God's command with Hitler-like efficiency. This made God angry with Saul, not because Saul killed too many but because Saul killed too few. Saul spared the King of the Amalekites and some of the livestock. For these acts of mercy, God removed Saul from being king.

This story calls into question some very basic and widespread beliefs about the Christian God.

• **Omnipotence.** Why was almighty God so afraid of little babies, "infants and sucklings", that he commanded that they all be murdered?

• **Mercy.** It is difficult to imagine something less merciful than genocide. Yet that is what God commanded the Israelites to do. When they did not kill enough people and even animals, God punished them for being merciful.

• **Justice.** God's own law, as well as common decency, prohibit killing anyone for the actions of their ancestors. Deuteronomy 24:16 says, "The fathers shall not be put to death for the children, **neither** shall the children be put to death for the fathers; every man shall be put to death for his own sin". But God commanded that every person in an entire nation be murdered because of something that their ancestors had done 400 years earlier.

• **Morality, wisdom and truth.** Wise, moral people do not commit genocide. If the Bible-God really stood for absolute truth, he would have figured out a way to help at least some of those little babies grow up and believe the truth so he wouldn't have to kill them.

God Punished The Wrong People Again, 40 Years Late

The books of Kings and Chronicles describe Josiah as the Hebrew king who was most devoted to God. 2 Kings 23:25 says, "Like unto him was there no king before him, that turned to the Lord with all his heart, and with all his soul, and with all his might, according to all the law of Moses; neither after him arose there any like him".

Nevertheless, God was angry and vowed to punish the Jews. The very next verses, 2 Kings 23:26-27 say, "Notwithstanding the Lord turned not from the fierceness of his great wrath, wherewith his anger was kindled against Judah, because of all the provocations that Manasseh had provoked him withal. And the Lord said, I will remove Judah also out of my sight, as I have removed Israel, and will cast off this city Jerusalem which I have chosen, and the house of which I said, My name shall be there."

One punishment was that God allowed Josiah to be killed in battle, according to 2 Kings 23:28-30 and 2 Chronicles 35:20-27.

Another punishment was that, "The Lord sent against him [Judah's king Jehoiakim, who reigned after Josiah died] bands of the Chaldees, and bands of the Syrians, and bands of the Moabites, and bands of the children of Ammon, and sent them against Judah to destroy it," according to 2 Kings 24:2.

Why was God upset? 2 Kings 24:3 provides this answer, "Surely at the commandment of the Lord came this upon Judah, to remove them out of his sight, for the sins of Manasseh, according to all that he did". The Bible specifically says that it was because of Manasseh's sins, no one else's, here and in 2 Kings 23:26-27, above.

There are several problems with this "explanation". First, God did not punish Manasseh; he punished Josiah and the rest of the people of Judah. Josiah was Manasseh's grandson. When God punished Josiah and the rest of the people of Judah, Manasseh had been dead for over 40 years.

Second, 2 Chronicles 33:11-20 clearly says that Manasseh had repented of his sins. 2 Chronicles 33:12 leaves no doubt that Manasseh was sincere: "He [Manasseh] besought the Lord his God, and humbled himself greatly before the God of his fathers". 2 Chronicles 33:13 is equally clear that God forgave Manasseh. "And [Manasseh] prayed unto him [God]: and he was intreated of him, and heard his supplication, and brought him again to Jerusalem into his kingdom. Then Manasseh knew that the Lord he was God".

God promised to forget people's sins when they repent. Isaiah 45:25 says, "I, even I, am he that blotteth out thy transgressions for mine own sake, and will not remember thy sins" (see also Isaiah 1:18 and Psalms 25:7). God broke this promise. God not only remembered Manasseh's sins for 2 generations after Manasseh repented, he then punished the wrong people, 40 years after Manasseh died.

An "Inspired" Book Of The Bible That Has No "Inspirer"?

Many Bible defenders use the Bible's own claims of divine inspiration to try to prove that the Bible is divinely inspired. This circular reasoning ignores the fact that other holy books, such as the Avesta and Baghavad-Gita, also claim to be inspired by the God(s) described therein. Some of these claims make the Bible's claims pale by comparison. Mormons believe that The Book of Mormon was brought to Earth directly from heaven on golden tablets and that it was translated into English with the help of miraculous eyeglasses. Non-Mormon Christians deride these claims, but accept the Bible's very similar (though less droll) claims by faith.

There is one book of the Bible, however, which undermines Christians' assertion that the whole Bible claims to be inspired by God.

The book of Esther does not mention God or prayer one single time. It implies an undefined influence on her destiny in Esther 4:14, and may indirectly refer to prayer in Esther 4:3 and 4:16, but it never specifically mentions either God or prayer.

Statistics on the book of Esther:

Name	Number of times mentioned in Esther
Esther	56
Mordecai	58
Ahasuerus, King of Persia	29 (Ahasuerus), 195 (king)
Haman	53
Queen Vashti	10
King Ahasuerus' Horse	1
Jehovah, The Lord, or God	ZERO
Angels	ZERO
Anyone you can pray to	ZERO
Prayer/praying	ZERO
Old Testament Law	ZERO

Not only does the book of Esther make no claim of divine inspiration or inerrancy, it does not even mention an inspirer or inerranter!

The book of Esther also says that Esther disobeyed Old Testament laws: she married a pagan (Ahasuerus) and lived as a pagan in his palace. Because she committed these sins, however, she was able to save the Jewish nation from annihilation.

Although the main theme of the book of Esther - the Jews' rescue from extermination - has not been corroborated by archeology or by ancient Persian historical records, Esther is a refreshing tribute to the wisdom and courage of women, in stark contrast to the many parts of the Bible that treat women as inferiors or worse. Esther has been enjoyed by supporters of women's rights, nervously worshipped by Bibliolaters, and ignored by most male Christians and Jews, ever since it was written.

Deals With The Devil

2 Peter 2:4 says, "God spared not the angels that sinned, but cast them down to hell, and delivered them into chains of darkness, to be reserved unto judgment". This belief is repeated in Jude 6, "the angels which kept not their first estate, but left their own habitation, he hath reserved in everlasting chains under darkness unto the judgment of the great day". If these verses were correct, 100% of demons, fallen angels and evil spirits would be locked up and could do us no harm.

But other Bible passages clearly say that many fallen angels were not cast "down to hell" or in "chains". They were, and presumably still are, free to roam the earth and make people miserable. A partial list of these passages includes: Genesis 6:2, Matthew 4:24, 8:16, 9:32, 12:22, 12:43-45, 15:22 and 17:15-18, Mark 1:21-27, 1:32, 1:34-39, 3:7-11, 6:13, 7:25-30, 9:17-27 and 16:17, Luke 4:33-36, 4:41, 6:17-18, 7:21, 8:2, 9:38-42, 11:14, 11:24-26 and 13:11, Acts 5:16, 16:16-18 and 19:12, 1 Corinthians 5:5 and 10:20-21, 2 Corinthians 11:14 and 12:7, Ephesians 6:11, 1 Timothy 3:7 and 4:1, and 1 Peter 5:8

It gets worse. The Bible says that almighty God had many opportunities to capture these evil spirits and did not do so. In Job chapters 1-2, God and Satan discussed ways to torture Job, and God allowed Satan to carry out his evil plans. Jesus and Satan met face to face in Matthew 4:1-10 and Luke 4:1-13, but Jesus did not lay a hand on him, even though Jesus claimed to have "all power" in Matthew 28:18.

When Jesus met the Gadarene(s) who were possessed by a "legion" of demons in Luke 8:26-36, Mark 5:1-13 and Matthew 8:28-34, he did not do what 2 Peter 2:4 and Jude 6 said he would do. Instead he did what the demons asked him to do! The demons "besought him that he would not command them to go out into the deep". So Jesus let them go into a herd of swine instead of casting them into hell.

It gets even worse. In 1 Kings 22:19-23 and 2 Chronicles 18:18-22, God wanted to kill king Ahab. So he asked "all the host of heaven" how to do it, and one of them suggested, "I will go out, and be a lying spirit in the mouth of all his prophets". When the lying spirit said that, he was standing "before the Lord". It would have been extremely easy for all-powerful God to immediately cast him down to hell as soon as he suggested that God take part in a lying scheme to get someone killed, which is two sins because lying is a sin and you are not supposed to tempt God (Deuteronomy 6:16, Matthew 4:7, James 1:13). But God commanded the spirit, "go out, and do even so". God commanded that spirit to sin. Then God let the lying spirit go to earth and commit that sin, resulting in a person getting killed.

God Lied And Lied And Lied

The Bible is adamantly against lying. Lying is forbidden in the Exodus 20 and Deuteronomy 5 versions of the Ten Commandments. Revelation 21:8 says, "all liars shall have their part in the lake which burneth with fire and brimstone, which is the second death". In John 8:44, Jesus said, "the devil ... was a murderer from the beginning, and abode not in the truth, because there is no truth in him. When he speaketh a lie, he speaketh of his own: for he is a liar, and the father of it."

John 14:6 claims that Jesus is the personification of truth, "I am ... the truth". Hebrews 6:18 says, "it was impossible for God to lie". If these statements are accurate, the number of times that we can catch Jehovah/Jesus in the actual act of lying should be precisely **zero**.

Nevertheless, the Bible clearly says that God is a very proficient and effective liar when it suits his purposes.

Ezekiel 14:9 says, "If the prophet be deceived when he hath spoken a thing, I the Lord have deceived that prophet, and I will stretch out my hand upon him, and will destroy him from the midst of my people Israel." If this is true, God deceived at least one prophet so that he could destroy him.

2 Thessalonians 2:11-12 says, "God shall send them strong delusion, that they should believe a lie: That they all might be damned, who believed not the truth, but had pleasure in unrighteousness". The Bible says that God deludes people, resulting in their damnation.

2 Chronicles 18:18-22 says that God wanted to kill someone, so he commanded a spirit to lie to provide an excuse for assassination. If this is true, God committed two sins: (1) anyone who commands someone to lie is at least as big a liar as the person he is telling to lie, and (2) lies are a sin, so God commanded the spirit to do something that would send the spirit to burn forever in Hell.

"Therefore hear the word of the Lord. I saw the Lord sitting upon his throne, and all the host of heaven standing on his right hand and on his left. And the Lord said, Who shall entice Ahab king of Israel, that he may go up and fall at Ramoth-gilead? And one spake saying after this manner, and another saying after that manner. Then there came out a spirit, and stood before the Lord, and said, I will entice him. And the Lord said unto him, Wherewith? And he said, I will go out, and be a lying spirit in the mouth of all his prophets. And the Lord said, Thou shalt entice him, and thou shalt also prevail: **go out, and do even so.** Now therefore, behold, **the Lord hath put a lying spirit in the mouth** of these thy prophets, and the Lord hath spoken evil against thee".

More Lies

As described on the preceding page, God's prohibitions against lying were no hindrance to himself telling some big whoppers when he wanted to. God's double standard goes beyond his own prevarications, however. The Bible gives many examples of God praising and/or rewarding his followers for lying, even if (often because) the lies were spoken with murderous intentions.

Judges 4:17-22 tells the story of Jael, a woman who offered to hide Sisera, captain of the Canaanite army, after he was defeated in battle. Jael lured Sisera into her tent by lying to him, "turn in to me, fear not" (verse 18). But when he fell asleep, she took a tent nail and, "smote the nail into his temples ... so he died". Jael was not punished. The prophetess Deborah gave Jael a special blessing in a bloodthirsty poem in Judges chapter 5: "Blessed above women shall Jael ... be" (verse 24).

1 Samuel 27:8-12 says that David lied to Achish, king of Gath, by telling him that he had been attacking the Hebrew tribe of Judah. David also committed genocide to cover up for his lie. Verses 8-12 say, "David and his men went up, and invaded the Geshurites, and the Gezrites, and the Amalekites ... David smote the land, and left neither man nor woman alive, Achish said, Whither have ye made a road to day? And David said, against the south of Judah, and against the south of the Jerahmeelites, and against the south of the Kenites. **David saved neither man nor woman alive, to bring tidings to Gath, saying, Lest they should tell on us**, saying, So did David, and so will be his manner all the while he dwelleth in the country of the Philistines. And Achish believed David, saying, He hath made his people Israel utterly to abhor him; therefore he shall be my servant for ever". David was never punished for this lie or the murders of any of the innocent people he killed to cover it up.

2 Kings chapter 10 says that Jehu lied so that he could kill some Baal worshippers. Verses 18-19 say, "And Jehu gathered all the people together, and said unto them, Ahab served Baal a little; but Jehu shall serve him much. Now therefore call unto me all the prophets of Baal, all his servants, and all his priests; let none be wanting: for I have a great sacrifice to do to Baal; whosoever shall be wanting, he shall not live. But Jehu did it in subtly, to the intent that he might destroy the worshippers of Baal." Verses 24-25 say that he ordered the Baal worshippers to be killed in their own temple.

Jehu made a bald-faced lie. But he had noble motives - at least by Biblical standards - to murder large numbers of people who had a politically incorrect religion. God was so pleased with Jehu's lies and murders that 2 Kings 10:30 says, "The Lord said unto Jehu, Because thou hast done well in executing that which is right in mine eyes, and hast done unto the house of Ahab according to all that was in mine heart, thy children of the fourth generation shall sit on the throne of Israel".

All Is Not All

The word "all" is a precise mathematical term. Mathematically, "all" and its synonyms "every", "everyone", "everything", "any", as well as similar but archaic words like "whosoever", mean that the items included in a set have no exceptions. We use this concept every day. If your employer says that "all" employees will get an increase in their salary, you will be looking for that money in your next paycheck.

"All" is also a precise legal term. When the United States Constitution says, "In all criminal prosecutions, the accused shall enjoy the right to a speedy and public trial, by an impartial jury", you and your lawyer know what that means.

"All" is a theological term which describes some of the most essential beliefs of all Christians. The most important, and anxiety-producing, of these doctrines is the belief that God will forgive "all" of the sins committed by Christians. If the Bible does not really mean "all" when it says "all", no Christian can ever be sure that God will forgive all of his/her sins. Since it only takes one sin to send you to Hell, no Christian would ever be able to be sure that they would go to Heaven.

The Greek word for "all" is "pas". The Hebrew word for "all" is "kol". Numerous Bible passages use "all" or one of its synonyms to assure Bible believers that every one of their sins are forgiven. Examples include:

- Psalm 103:3 - God "forgiveth all [kol] thine iniquities"
- Proverbs 10:12 - "love covereth all [kol] sins"
- Acts 13:39 - "by him [Jesus] all [pas] that believe are justified from all [pas] things"
- Psalm 145:20 - "The Lord preserveth all [kol] them that love him"
- 1 John 1:9 - "If we confess our sins, he is faithful and just to forgive us our sins, and to cleanse us from all [pas] unrighteousness"
- 1 John 1:7 - "If we walk in the light, as he is in the light ... the blood of Jesus Christ his Son cleanseth us from all [pas] sin"

The above passages notwithstanding, many other Bible passages cast doubt on whether God really means what he says when he says "all".

The very first chapter of the Bible tells us that all is not all. Genesis 1:31 says, "God saw every [kol] thing that he had made, and, behold, it was very good". But Genesis chapter 3 says that the Devil was definitely not good.

In Genesis 22:18 and 26:4, God said to Abraham, "in thy seed shall all [kol] the nations of the earth be blessed". But other Bible verses clearly say that some nations were definitely **not** blessed by Abraham's descendants. They were genocidally exterminated at God's command. Some of these are described in "God Ordered > 3,000,000 Violations Of 'Thou Shalt Not Murder'" on page 54 of this book.

(continued on next page)

Did God really mean it when he said, "David did that which was right in the eyes of the Lord, and turned not aside from any [kol] thing that he commanded him all [kol] the days of his life, save only in the matter of Uriah the Hittite" in 1 Kings 15:5? This is the same David who sexually mutilated 200 corpses in 1 Samuel 18:20-27. David committed genocide against the Geshurites, Gezrites, and Amalekites in 1 Samuel 27:8-12, Moabites in 2 Samuel 8:2 and Edomites in 1 Kings 11:15-16. David ordered the slaughter of people with disabilities 2 Samuel 5:7-10 and tortured people with saws in 1 Chronicles 20:3.

One of Jesus' more famous sayings is in Matthew 26:52, "All [pas] they that take the sword shall perish with the sword". But Moses, Joshua, David and Jehu did an awful lot of killing and died peacefully. For more information, see "Not all that take the sword shall perish with the sword" on page 7 of this book.

Another example is the Unpardonable Sin, described in Mark 3:29, Luke 12:10 and Matthew 12:31-32, which says, "Wherefore I [Jesus] say unto you, All manner of sin and blasphemy shall be forgiven unto men: but the blasphemy against the Holy Ghost shall not be forgiven unto men. ... whosoever speaketh against the Holy Ghost, it shall not be forgiven him, neither in this world, neither in the world to come." Christian theologians disagree about just what you have to do to commit the Unpardonable Sin. Although God won't tell his own experts what constitutes the Unpardonable Sin, if you commit one, you're doomed.

Colossians 3:20 commands, "Children, obey your parents in all [pas] things". This is another verse where "all" clearly does not mean "all". Children are not obligated to steal, lie, murder or commit idolatry even if their parent commands them to do so. Nor are children required to endure gross neglect, sexual abuse or other kinds of physical or psychological abuse.

Titus 2:9 commands, "Exhort servants to be obedient unto their own masters, and to please them well in all [pas] things". The word translated "servants" in this verse is "doulos" and means "slaves". The most obvious problem with this passage is that many male and female slaves were commanded by their masters to be prostitutes. Was Paul really telling slaves to commit adultery/fornication with dozens of different people every day if their master told them to "please them well"? If so, he contradicted 1 Thessalonians 4:3, "For this is the will of God, even your sanctification, that ye should abstain from fornication".

The most extreme example of "All Is Not All" is God's claim in John 3:16 that he loves the whole "world". But other Bible verses make it clear that he will send the vast majority of humanity to burn forever in Hell.

Not Is Not Not

The word "not" is a precise mathematical term and is an essential part of other precise mathematical terms. "Not" negates a condition, such as "not less than". It also excludes items from a set, e.g., "not for sale". The mathematical term "not equal" is almost as ubiquitous as the mathematical term "equal". Just about every computer programming language contains a symbol or keyword for "not". If it were not for "not", it would not be possible to calculate a paycheck or perform many other mathematically simple functions that we take for granted.

The Bible contains a multitude of "nots" - over 2,600 in the King James translation - not counting similar words like "no", "none", "neither" or "nor", which mean "not" in some contexts. God's second command to mankind was, "of the tree of the knowledge of good and evil, thou shalt not eat" (Genesis 2:17). Nine out of the Ten Commandments (Exodus 20 and Deuteronomy 5 versions) use "no" or "not".

You would think that with all that practice, Jehovah and Jesus would have figured out what us mere humans know - that "not" really does mean "not". Unfortunately, this is not the case, which has enormous theological significance. If God did not always mean "not" when he said "not", we can not know for sure what God has prohibited, which could have serious, fatal or even eternal consequences.

The most obviously contradictory "not" in the Bible is God's commandment, "Thou Shalt Not Kill", in Exodus 20:13 and Deuteronomy 5:17. God repeatedly contradicted this prohibition by requiring his followers to kill large numbers of unbelievers, including noncombatant women, children and little babies, and even many Hebrews whom he disapproved of. This created "Unavoidable Sins" for God's followers: obeying God's commandment not to kill would have violated his frequent commands to commit brutal mass murders, and vice versa. Some of these genocides are described elsewhere in this book; see Chapter 3, "God Ordered > 3,000,000 Violations Of 'Thou Shalt Not Murder'" and "God 'Takes Care Of' > 30,000 Widows And Orphans" and Chapter 5, "God Punished The Wrong People, Hundreds Of Years Late".

I Corinthians 13:4 says that love is not jealous. The King James Bible is archaic, "charity envieth **not**"; modern translations are more direct. The Weymouth translation says, "love knows **neither** envy **nor** jealousy". Most other modern translations say something similar. But God said repeatedly that he was in fact jealous. In two versions of the Ten Commandments, God said, "I the Lord thy God am a jealous God" (Exodus 20:5 and Deuteronomy 5:9). Deuteronomy 4:24 says, "The Lord thy God is a consuming fire, even a jealous God". Exodus 34:14 says, "The Lord, whose name is Jealous, is a jealous God".

(continued on next page)

Many Bible passages clearly ascribe to God many characteristics of extreme jealousy which would be deeply pathological in a human. Jealous people often demand impossible levels of conformity and perfectionism; God does this in Matthew 5:48 and Deuteronomy 18:13. Jealous people frequently use fear and threats to obtain obedience; God does this in Deuteronomy 6:2, 6:13, 6:24 and 28:15-68. Jealous people often give punishments which are much worse than the offenses; God did this in Matthew 5:22, Leviticus 26:18 and Numbers 11:1. Pathologically jealous people use threats of physical violence against people that they "love"; God did this in Exodus 22:24, Leviticus 26:16-30, Deuteronomy 8:19-20, Ezekiel 23:25-26, Zephaniah 1:18 and 3:8, 1 Corinthians 5:5, 11:29-30, Philippians 3:18-19 and with his many threats of making people burn forever in Hell, e.g., Matthew 10:28. In extreme cases, a very sick form of jealousy can cause the jealous person to commit physical violence against the people they "love", up to and including murder; God did this in Exodus 32:27-35, Psalm 79:1-5 and Ezekiel 16:38. If God is that jealous, and love is not jealous, it cannot truly be said that God loves his followers, except in a very sick way.

Does God repent? Numbers 23:19 says "God is **not**...the son of man, that he should repent". The Hebrew word translated "repent" is "nacham". But the Bible says many times that God does "nacham". Genesis 6:6-7 says twice that God "repented" (nacham) that he had made the entire human race. God also repented in Exodus 32:12-14, Judges 2:17-18, Jonah 3:10 and 4:2, Amos 7:3 and 7:6, and 2 Samuel 2:30-31.

1 Samuel 15:29 says that God, "will **not** lie or repent [nacham], for he is **not** a man that he should repent [nacham]". But in 1 Samuel 15:11, God said, "It repenteth [nacham] me that I have set up Saul to be king". 1 Samuel 15:35 says, "the Lord repented [nacham] that he had made Saul king". Twice in chapter 15 we are told that God does not repent; twice in that same chapter we are told that God does repent.

Deuteronomy 24:16 contradicts one of Christianity's most important doctrines: the belief that Jesus died for people's sins. It says, "The fathers shall **not** be put to death for the children ... every man shall be put to death for his own sin". It contradicts the belief that Jesus died for people's sins because:
• Jesus is God, John 1:1, John 10:30
• God is our father, Matthew 6:9, 2 Corinthians 6:18
• Fathers cannot legally die for their children's sins, Deuteronomy 24:16
Therefore it would be a violation of God's own law for Jesus to die for people's sins. According to Matthew 5:17 and Galatians 3:13, Jesus supposedly fulfilled the penalties required by God's Law by dying for people's sins. But Jesus actually broke God's Law by doing so. You can not break a law and fulfill it at the same time.

Forever Is Not Forever

"Forever" is a precise mathematical term meaning "for an infinite length of time". The question of whether the Universe will last forever or eventually collapse and repeat another "Big Bang" is one of the most important issues in Cosmology. Technologically advanced nations are spending many billions of dollars to develop space probes and huge telescopes which may help to answer this question.

There is enormous theological importance to the word "forever" because it is the basis for Christians' belief that they will live forever in Heaven with God. John 12:25 says, "He that hateth his life in this world shall keep it unto life eternal". Matthew 19:29 says, "Every one that hath forsaken houses, or brethren, or sisters, or father, or mother, or wife, or children, or lands, for my name's sake, shall receive an hundredfold, and shall inherit everlasting life".

Christians make enormous sacrifices of "time, talent and treasure" because God commanded them to, "lay up for yourselves treasures in Heaven" in Matthew 6:20. To Christians, it is absolutely essential that the Bible-God meant what he said when he promised that they would live forever. Anything that casts doubt on that belief removes the biggest reason why many Christians are Christians.

Casting doubt on this belief is exactly what the Bible does.

Psalm 78:69 says, "He [God] built his sanctuary like high palaces, like the earth which he hath established for ever". The Hebrew word translated "for ever" in this verse is "olam". It is also used in Psalm 104:5, "[God] Who laid the foundations of the earth, that it should not be removed for ever [olam]". Ecclesiastes 1:4 says, "the earth abideth for ever [olam]".

But other passages in the Bible very clearly contradict the idea that "for ever" means "for ever" when describing the earth's future. Jesus himself said, "Heaven and earth shall pass away" in Matthew 24:35, Mark 13:31 and Luke 21:33. 2 Peter 3:10-13 says that the earth will be "burned up". Isaiah 65:17 says, "I [God]create new heavens and a new earth, and the former shall not be remembered, nor come into mind". So "olam" is **not** "forever".

The Bible repeatedly uses "olam" in its claims about God. Psalm 136 says 26 times that God's, "mercy endureth for ever [olam]". Psalm 111:9 says that God "commanded his covenant for ever [olam]". Psalm 146:10 says, "The Lord shall reign for ever". Isaiah 40:8 says, "The grass withers, the flower fades, but the word of our God shall stand for ever [olam]".

Other passages give good reasons to doubt whether God's "olam" is a long time. Psalm 136:10 says, "To him that smote Egypt in their firstborn: for his mercy endureth for ever [olam]". This is a reference to Exodus 12:29, which says, "At

(continued on next page)

midnight the Lord smote all the firstborn in the land of Egypt, from the firstborn of Pharoah that sat on his throne unto the firstborn of the captive that was in the dungeon; and all the firstborn of cattle". Psalm 136:10 is a blatant contradiction even by Biblical standards - a verse that contradicts itself. God killed hundreds of thousands of people in a single night, the vast majority of whom were children and poor peasants, few if any of whom had the slightest influence over Pharaoh's decision to keep the Israelites in Egypt. To those unfortunate Egyptians, God's mercy did not last "for ever"; it did not even last one night.

Psalm 30:5 says, "For his [God's] anger endureth but a moment". The Hebrew word translated "anger" in this verse is "aph". Psalm 103:8-9 says, "The Lord is merciful and gracious, slow to anger [aph], and plenteous in mercy. He will not always chide, neither will he keep his anger [aph] for ever [olam]". But in Jeremiah 17:4, God said, "Ye have kindled a fire in mine anger [aph], which shall burn for ever [olam]". Malachi 1:4 says that the Edomites are, "The people against whom the Lord hath indignation for ever [olam]".

Daniel 12:2 says, "And many of them that sleep in the dust of the earth shall awake, some to everlasting [olam] life, and some to shame and everlasting [olam] contempt". This verse supports some of Bible believers' most cherished doctrines: eternal life and eternal damnation. But other Bible verses deny that we exist after death. Isaiah 26:14 says, "They are dead, they shall not live; they are deceased, they shall not rise: therefore hast thou visited and destroyed them, and made all their memory to perish". Job 7:9 says, "As the cloud is consumed and vanishes away, so he that goeth down to the grave shall come up no more". Psalm 6:5 says, "For in death there is no remembrance of thee: in the grave who shall give thee thanks?" Psalm 115:17 says, "The dead praise not the Lord, neither any that go down into silence". Ecclesiastes 9:5 says, "The dead know not anything, neither have they any more a reward".

Numbers 18:6-8 requires that only members of the tribe of Levi can offer sacrifices "for ever" [olam]. But 1 Samuel 1:1 and 1:20 say that Samuel was a member of the tribe of Ephraim; he offered a sacrifice to God in 1 Samuel 7:9. God showed his approval of Samuel's behavior by giving the Israelites several military victories in 1 Samuel 7:10-14 and making Samuel the judge of Israel "all the days of his life", according to 1 Samuel 7:15.

Deuteronomy 23:3 says, "A ... Moabite shall not enter into the congregation of the Lord, even to their tenth generation ... for ever [olam]". But Ruth 4:13-17 and Matthew 1:5 say that King David was the great-grandson of Ruth, who was a Moabite. David did much more than "enter the congregation", he was king. He also wrote over seventy Psalms.

Chapter 6

Scientific and Geometrical Math Mistakes

Bible believers are quick to point out that the Bible is not a scientific book. But they are just as quick to claim that the Bible's "scientific" statements are as infallible as the rest of the Bible. This statement is actually quite correct - the Bible's scientific and geometrical statements are every bit as underliable as its other claims.

Bible believers usually rationalize by saying something like "faith is a different kind of knowing", i.e., science, math, history, etc., are based on evidence, but religious "truth" has a different basis. There are several problems with this idea:

• Christians repeatedly claim that there is hard evidence for their faith, although only a very few can provide any. Even then, if you ask probing questions about their "evidence", they are quick to point out that you are a depraved sinner (or are risking losing your eternal salvation if you are a Christian) and if you just had more faith then you would be convinced by their "evidence". Christians usually get offended if you say that they have blind faith, but Appendix 2 demonstrates that the Bible teaches exactly that - Christian faith is blind; the blinder the better.

• Christians have used their beliefs to influence public policy for almost 1,700 years. In modern times, Christians use their beliefs to restrict legitimate scientific research, force their beliefs on others in public schools, deprive women of reproductive freedom and use government funds to promote narrow sectarian views. If Christians are going to use their beliefs as an excuse to use the power of government to force those beliefs on non-Christians, those beliefs must be subject to public, factual debate on the same basis as any other means of influencing public policy.

• Believers in Hinduism, Islam, Wicca and thousands of other religions are just as strongly convinced of the absolute, exclusive truth of their religious beliefs as Christians are. If religious faith is not based on objective evidence, there is no way to be certain that your faith is the correct one until you die and then it is too late.

• Science has corrected many theological errors. Christians used to believe that the earth was the center of the universe, that epilepsy and mental illness were caused by demon possession, that plagues were punishment from God and that lightning was a weapon of Satan. Science has not only corrected these incorrect beliefs, it has given us ways to counteract the effects of the human tragedies that these erroneous beliefs attempted to explain but did not prevent or mitigate, and in many cases actually made worse.

Jesus said, "Blessed are they that have not seen, and yet have believed" (John 20:29). Science empowers you to see for yourself.

Why Can We See Stars That Are > 10,000 Light Years Away?

If you add up the "begats" in the Old Testament, you can calculate the Biblical date of the creation of the Universe. Christian conservatives usually claim this date is 4004 BCE. Orthodox Jews usually claim that this date is 3761 BCE. (This disagreement is evidence that the Bible contradicts itself about this all-important date.) There is no other date for the Creation that can be calculated from the Bible that is substantially older than either of these dates.

One light year is the distance that a photon of light travels in the vacuum of space in one year. Modern telescopes can see galaxies that are over 10 billion light years away, enabling astronomers to create 3-dimensional maps of much of our own galaxy, as well as larger structures such as our Local Group of galaxies and even the large scale structure of the observable Universe.

How do we know how far away a star or galaxy is? There are at least four ways: parallax, cepheid variables, type 1a supernovas and redshifts. There are many books which describe and prove these highly reliable scientific techniques[1]. Genesis literalists rarely understand any of these methods; the few that do reject them by faith.

Suffice it to say that an enormous amount of hard scientific evidence supports the fact that telescopes enable us to see billions of galaxies and millions of individual stars that are many times farther away than 10,000 light years.

If Genesis was literally true, we would not be able to see these far-distant celestial objects. In fact, we would see stars, approximately 6,000 light-years distant, winking into existence at the moment of creation. You could literally prove the existence of God and the truth of the Bible, and watch the first two chapters of Genesis happen over and over, with an inexpensive telescope that would fit in your knapsack. Unfortunately for Genesis literalists, this is not the way the Universe works.

The Andromeda Galaxy is 2,500,000 light years from Earth. On a moonless night and away from city lights, most people can see it with their unaided eyes if they know where to look. It is easier to see with a small telescope or binoculars. You can find Andromeda's location online or on commercially available star charts. So now you know how to look up into the night sky and see with your own eyes that the Genesis creation did not happen!

Genesis believers usually try to explain this by saying that God created a Universe that appears to be is much older than it really is. If so, God has created a lie of gargantuan proportions. It is difficult to explain why God would go to such great lengths to deceive people when he claims that he wants everyone to know the truth. It is even more difficult to claim that God stands for truth or morality if he has created the biggest lie in the Universe - the Universe itself.

Only Three Guys Noticed A Low-Flying Star

One of the most famous Bible stories is in Matthew 2:1-9.

"When Jesus was born in Bethlehem of Judea in the days of Herod the king, ... there came wise men from the east to Jerusalem, Saying, 'Where is he that is born King of the Jews? For we have seen his star in the east, and are come to worship him'. When Herod the king had heard these things, he was troubled, and all Jerusalem with him ... the star, which they saw in the east, went before them, till it came and stood over where the young child was."

Any object in the sky that appeared to "go before" anyone on the ground who was travelling from Jerusalem to Bethlehem (a distance of about 5 miles), then appeared to "stand over" something as small as an individual residence, could not have been more than a few thousand feet in the air. If this had been a real star, it would have vaporized the entire Earth long before it got that close.

Bible believers explain away this problem by saying it was a miraculous star. But there are problems with this story that a miraculous star cannot explain.

When the wise men told Herod about the star, "he was troubled, and all Jerusalem with him". Even if the Jews in Jerusalem had not noticed the star, Matthew assures us that large numbers of them certainly knew about it at that time, **before** the star led the wise men to Bethlehem.

These Jews had been eagerly awaiting the Messiah/Christ for centuries. Here was a star announcing the arrival of the Messiah!! If "all Jerusalem" actually knew about the "star", which really "stood over where the young child [Jesus] was", the wise men would have been accompanied by an enormous throng of Jews while the "star" led them all to Jesus. This would have been extremely powerful eyewitness evidence of Jesus' divinity, yet there is no mention of this multitude of Jews in the Bible.

After the star led them to Jesus, the wise men, Joseph, Mary and Jesus were able to leave secretly. This would have been impossible if "all Jerusalem" had heard about the wise men's explanation of the star's Messianic significance.

This is another evolving myth in the Bible. The Apostles in the book of Acts tried very hard to convince people of Jesus' divinity, yet there is no mention of the Messianic star which would surely have been seen by some witnesses who were still living in Jerusalem. The letters attributed to the Apostle Paul claim that there were many witnesses to the resurrected Jesus, but never once mention witnesses to the star. But the Gospel of Matthew, which many Bible scholars believe was written much later, reports that a star announced Jesus' birth, just as stars had announced the births of Horus[2], Buddha[3] and Krishna[4], many centuries before the New Testament was written.

More Misplaced Stars

Genesis 1:6-8 says, "God said, Let there be a firmament in the midst of the waters, and let it divide the waters from the waters. And God made the firmament, and divided the waters which were under the firmament from the waters which were **above** the firmament, and it was so. And God called the firmament Heaven".

Note that Genesis says that there were "waters which were **above** the firmament". This is a poetic way of saying that God created a "firmament" to separate the "waters" in the lakes, rivers and oceans from the "waters" in the clouds in the sky.

Genesis 1:14-15 tells us more about the "firmament". "God said, Let there be lights **in** the firmament of the heaven to divide the day from the night; and let them be for signs, and for seasons, and for days, and years. And let them be for lights **in** the firmament of the heaven to give light upon the earth: and it was so. And God made two great lights; the greater light to rule the day, and the lesser light to rule the night: he made the stars also. And God set them **in** the firmament of the heaven to give light upon the earth". Note that Genesis says that the stars are **in** the firmament.

Scholars have debated for centuries what a "firmament" is. The Hebrew word is "raqia", which some Bibles translate as "expanse". Whatever it is, the Bible says that the clouds are **above** the firmament/expanse and every extraterrestrial light is **in** it. The stars, moon and sun are above the clouds; Genesis is just plain wrong.

*   *   *

Did God Create Man Or The Animals First?

One simple but important historical, scientific and mathematical concept is that time flows in one direction - forward. If event "A" follows event "B", then event "A" cannot also precede event "B".

Genesis 1:20-25 says that God created all of the animals on land and sea. "God created great whales, and every living creature that moveth, which the waters brought forth abundantly, after their kind, and every winged fowl after his kind ... the evening and the morning were the fifth day ... God made the beast of the earth after his kind, and cattle after their kind, and every thing that creepeth upon the earth".

After that, Genesis 1:27 says, "God created man in his own image, in the image of God created he him; male and female created he them".

But Genesis 2:7 says that God created man before he created the animals, "The Lord God formed man of the dust of the ground, and breathed into his nostrils the breath of life; and man became a living soul". Twelve verses later, in Genesis 2:19, God created the animals, "Out of the ground the Lord God formed every beast of the field and every fowl of the air".

Wrong By Hundreds Of Miles Per Second

We now know that the Earth rotates on its axis once every day and orbits the sun at a speed of about 580,000,000 miles per year. Our solar system orbits the center of our galaxy at over 6,400,000,000 miles per year. Our galaxy is zipping away from almost every other known galaxy at a substantial percentage of the speed of light.

These facts were unknown to the Bible's authors, who repeatedly and dogmatically stated that the Earth does not move. 1 Chronicles 16:30 says, "Fear before him [God], all the earth: the world also shall be stable, that it be not moved". Psalm 93:1 says, "The world also is stablished, that it cannot be moved". Psalm 96:10 says, "The Lord reigneth, the world also shall be established that it shall not be moved". Psalm 33:8-9 says, "Let all the earth fear the Lord. Let all the inhabitants of the world stand in awe of him. For he spake, and it was done; he commanded, and it stood fast". The Hebrew word translated "stood fast" in Psalm 33:9 is "amad". Amad is used hundreds of times in the Old Testament; every single time it means "stay in one place".

The theory of the heliocentric solar system - that the earth and planets orbit the sun - was first published by in 1541 by Copernicus, who escaped persecution because he died that same year. The church executed Giordano Bruno for making this claim. Had Galileo not recanted, the church would have executed him too. When the church condemned Galileo, part of the condemnation read:

> "The proposition that the sun is the center of the world and does not move
> from its place is absurd and false philosophy and formally heretical, because
> it is expressly contrary to Holy Scripture. The proposition that the earth is not
> the center of the world and immovable, but that it moves, and also with a di-
> urnal motion [i.e., daily rotation], is equally absurd and false philosophically,
> and theologically, at least erroneous in faith"[5].

Leading Protestant theologians also condemned the theory of the heliocentric solar system. Martin Luther banned Copernicus' theories from being taught at Wittenburg University[6] and ridiculed him as an "upstart astrologer" and "fool" because "sacred Scripture tells us that Joshua commanded the sun to stand still, not the earth"[6]. The last quote is reference to Joshua 10:12-13, "He said in the sight of Israel, Sun, stand thou still upon Gibeon, and thou, Moon, in the valley of Ajalon. And the sun stood still, and the moon stayed".

In the mid-1700's, long after Kepler had conclusively proven the heliocentric solar system and Newton had quantified laws of physics to explain it, John Wesley, founder of the Methodist church, declared that it "tends toward infidelity"[6].

The Earth Hangs, Or It Sits On Pillars, Or On Heaping Seas

Job 26:7 says that God, "hangeth the earth upon nothing". Some modern Bible defenders claim that this verse means that the earth is in orbit. But the Hebrew word translated "hang" in this verse is "talah", the same word used to describe executing someone by hanging them on a tree in Genesis 40:19-23, Deuteronomy 21:22, Joshua 8:29 and 10:26, 2 Samuel 4:12, 21:12, Esther 6:4, 7:9-10, 8:7, and 9:14. "Talah" is used for hanging harps on trees in Psalm 137:2. Isaiah 22:23-25 uses "talah" for hanging things, "as a nail in a sure place". "Talah" means that something that "hangs" is not going anywhere; its location is stationary specifically because it is hanging.

No Bible scholar interpreted "hangeth" to mean "orbit" until long after science had forced Christian theologians to admit that the solar system was heliocentric. The great 16th century Protestant theologian John Calvin, in his commentary on Psalm 93:1, said, "How could the earth hang suspended in the air were it not upheld by God's hand? By what means could it maintain itself unmoved, while the heavens are in constant rapid motion, did not its divine maker fix and establish it?"

Other Bible verses claim with equal certainty that the Earth does **not** hang. Job 9:6 and Psalm 75:3 say that the Earth has "pillars". In Job 38:4-6, God said, "Where wast thou when I laid the foundations of the earth? Declare, if thou hast understanding. Who hath laid the measures thereof, if thou knowest? Or who hath stretched the line upon it? Whereupon are the foundations thereof fastened? Or who laid the corner stone thereof?

Still other passages claim that the Earth is founded upon seas. Psalm 24:1-2 says, "The earth is the Lord's ... For he hath founded it upon the seas". Psalm 136:6 claims that God, "stretched out the earth above the waters". This would appear quite obvious to someone who noticed that seas filled the lowest observable places in their area, but it indicates a complete ignorance of gravity and geology.

Psalm 33:7 says, "He [God] gathereth the waters of the sea together as an heap". In his commentary on Psalm 33:7, Calvin said, "Natural philosophers confess, and experience openly proclaims, that the waters occupy a **higher** place than the earth. How is it then that, as they are fluid and naturally disposed to flow, they do not spread abroad and cover the earth, and how is it that the earth, which is lower in position, remains dry? In this we certainly perceive God, who is ever attentive to the welfare of the human race, has enclosed the waters within certain invisible barriers, and keeps them shut up to this day, and the prophet elegantly declares that they stand still at God's commandment, as if they were a heap of solid matter".

If God had really invented hydrology, he would have revealed more of it to the Bible's authors and to his favorite theologians.

Stationary Sun And Moon

Joshua 10:12-14 says,

"Then spake Joshua to the Lord in the day when the Lord delivered up the Amorites before the children of Israel, and he said in the sight of Israel, Sun, stand thou still upon Gibeon; and thou, Moon, in the valley of Ajalon. And the sun stood still and the moon stayed, until the people had avenged themselves upon their enemies ... So the sun stood still in the midst of heaven, and hasted not to go down about a whole day. And there was no day like that before it or after it".

As previously noted in "Wrong By Hundreds Of Miles Per Second", this passage used to be regarded by Christian theologians as indisputable proof that the sun orbited a stationary Earth once each day. Although science (not Jesus) has corrected that "misinterpretation", many conservative Christians now believe that God miraculously stopped the earth's rotation and started it again a day later.

The earth rotates at over 1,000 miles per hour at the equator. If Joshua 10:12-14 is literally true, God stopped the earth and everything on it, including the oceans and atmosphere. He stopped the moon in its orbit and held it in place so it would not crash into the earth. After Joshua's army had killed enough Amorites, God then accelerated things back to normal "a whole day" later.

According to the Biblical chronology, this happened about 1500-1300 BCE, when Egyptian, Chinese, and Mesopotamian societies were well established. There is no way they could have failed to notice this 36 hour day. But there is no mention of it in their writings or other records, or those of any other ancient culture.

Why Did Satan Attack Church Steeples And Belfries?

Before modern times, Christians believed that the Devil could send lightning, based on Jesus' statement in Luke 10:18, "I beheld Satan as lightning fall from heaven". They also believed that God often sent lightning strikes, based on many passages including but not limited to Exodus 19:16, Job 28:26, 37:3, 38:25 and 38:35, Psalm 18:14, 77:18, 97:4, 135:7 and 144:6, Revelation 4:5, 8:5, 11:5 and 16:18.

This belief was supported by hard evidence that was as irrefutable as it was dramatic: the fact that churches were very often struck by lightning. Since most churches were made mostly or entirely of wood, lightning strikes were often extremely destructive and tragic.

Lightning that struck churches frequently left surrounding buildings untouched. In addition, these lightning strikes often targeted the holiest parts of the church: the steeple, which was the part of the church that was closest to God, and the bell tower, which contained the sanctified bells that called people to worship services and announced holy days. All of this was further proof that Satan was the culprit.

An alternative, but even more terrifying, explanation was that God was displeased with some people in that particular church and sent lightning to punish them.

In order to prevent these attacks, believers often appealed to God for protection. One method was to send someone up into the bell tower to ring the bells during thunderstorms. This was so common that 120 men were killed by lightning while ringing church bells during storms in just one Christian nation - Germany - over one short time period - from 1750 to 1783[7].

Today, we know that lightning strikes have nothing to do with religion. Churches are struck simply because they are often taller than nearby objects. God failed to mention this simple life-saving geometrical/scientific concept in the Bible.

It was not until that non-Christian Freethinker Benjamin Franklin invented the lightning rod in 1752 that churches and all other buildings could finally be protected from lightning. Although Franklin's invention was labelled "the heretical rod" and many churches initially resisted for theological reasons, within a few decades virtually all churches had accepted the scientific view of lightning and installed lightning rods, much to the relief of bell ringers everywhere[7].

Psalm 135:7 claims that God understands lightning, "He [God] maketh lightnings for the rain". Lightning rods are simple devices made of copper, bronze, brass or even iron; they could easily have been made in Biblical times and protected churches and synagogues for over 2,000 years, preventing the destruction of many holy places and saving many lives. If God has known all about lightning for thousands of years, why did he never get around to telling his followers how to protect themselves and their places of worship?

If I Ever Have Heart Surgery, Please Do Not Pray For Me

Psalm 103:2-3 says, "Bless the Lord, O my soul, and forget not all his benefits ... who healeth all thy diseases". James 5:14-15 says, "Is any sick among you? Let him call for the elders of the church; and let them pray over him, anointing him with oil in the name of the Lord, and the prayer of faith shall save the sick". John 14:13-14 says, "Whatsoever ye shall ask in my [Jesus'] name, that will I do ... If ye shall ask any thing in my name, I will do it".

If prayer works like the Bible says it does, the effects would be very easily detected by the same scientific methods that are used to test drugs and medical devices. Recently, over a dozen scientific studies have tried to do this.

Lancet is one of medicines' most prestigious journals. On July 16, 2005, on pages 211-217, it published the results of a study comparing the outcomes of prayer on 749 patients who received cardiac bypass surgery. The study concluded, "No significant differences were found" between the group that was prayed for and those who did not receive study-prescribed prayer.

The American Heart Journal is another well-respected medical journal. In April, 2006, on pages 934-942, it published a study involving 1,802 cardiac bypass surgery patients who were divided into three groups: one received no study-prescribed prayer, another group was prayed for but were not told about it and a third group was told that they were being prayed for. All of the people doing the study-sponsored praying were Christians. Not only did the prayed-for groups do no better than those who were not prayed for, those who were told that they were being prayed for did **worse** than those who received no study-sponsored prayer at all!

Meta Analysis combines the results of many different studies to reach a conclusion based on a large amount of data produced by many different researchers in many different geographical areas and situations. In August, 2006, the Annals of Behavioral Medicine published a Meta Analysis of 14 studies on prayer and healing. This Meta Analysis determined: "There is no scientifically discernable effect for IP [intercessory prayer] as assessed in controlled studies".

If prayer works the way that the Bible says it does, the effects would be profound. It would not take controlled scientific studies to prove it. But if anyone did do a study, the evidence would be overwhelming.

If prayer works, hospitals with large percentages of Christian staffs and patients would get dramatically better results than other hospitals. This just isn't so. Any religious hospital that made such a claim would be sued for slander by nearby non-religious hospitals if the non-religious hospitals could stop laughing long enough to do so. Actually, if prayer worked like the Bible says it does, Christians would not need hospitals at all.

Longevity And Christianity

Psalm 55:23 says, "Bloody and deceitful men shall not live out half their days". Imagine the enormous savings to our prisons if Psalm 55:23 was true! Instead of spending billions of dollars on life sentences for murderers and rapists until they live into their 70's, most of them would die before they reached their mid-40's.

Psalm 55:23 is poetic hyperbole and was never meant to be mathematically precise. But it is just one of many Bible passages which claim that God's followers live longer than other people do. Proverbs 10:27 says, "The fear of the Lord prolongeth days, but the years of the wicked shall be shortened". Proverbs 4:10-11 says, "Hear, O my son, and receive my sayings; and the years of thy life shall be many. I have taught thee in the way of wisdom". Deuteronomy 7:15 says, "The Lord will take away from thee all sickness, and will put none of the evil diseases of Egypt, which thou knowest, upon thee, but will lay them upon all them that hate thee".

This idea that God causes his followers to live longer than unbelievers is one of the most thoroughly disproven beliefs in modern times. From pre-history through Biblical times until the beginning of the Enlightenment in the 1700's, most people died in infancy or childhood, the vast majority of people died from diseases we rarely even hear about today, and people often died of old age in their 40's and 50's. Then humanity developed rational methods of preventing and treating disease, causing average human longevity to triple by the 21st century; it is still increasing.

This dramatic **in**crease in human longevity has been accompanied by a dramatic **de**crease in the percentage of Christians. Instead of relying on God to protect their health, people are getting vaccinated, practicing proper sanitation and taking their medicine, so most people are living much longer.

Modern health care works just as well for Bible believers as it does for Hindus, Muslims, Buddhists and nonreligious people. Unlike the Bible-God, science does not discriminate.

Pi And The "Molten Sea" In The Jerusalem Temple

1 Kings 7:23-26 and 2 Chronicles 4:2-5 describe a large brass or bronze basin, often translated "molten sea", in the Temple that held water which was used for ritual purifications. These descriptions contradict each other and even contradict themselves.

These two passages contradict each other because they give very different volumes for the molten sea. 1 Kings 7:26 says, "it contained **two** thousand baths". 2 Chronicles 4:5 says, "it received and held **three** thousand baths".

It is often noted that these passages also contain an incorrect value for Pi (π), which, rounded to two decimals, is 3.14. 1 Kings 7:23 says, "he made a molten sea, **ten** cubits from the one brim to the other: it was round all about, his height was **five** cubits: and a line of **thirty** cubits did compass it round about". 2 Chronicles 4:2 says something very similar. If the molten sea was 10 cubits in diameter, its circumference would have been over 31.4 cubits. Some commentators, however, have pointed out that 1 Kings 7:26 says that the walls of the basin were "an hand breadth thick", so if you measured the diameter on the **in**side of the basin and the circumference on the **out**side of it, you would have gotten relatively close to 3.14 for π. Whether or not the authors of Kings and Chronicles ever thought of this is debatable, but there are more serious geometrical problems with these passages.

The volume of the molten sea can be easily calculated from the dimensions provided in 1 Kings 7:23 (see above) and 1 Chronicles 4:2. It was round, 10 cubits in diameter and 5 cubits high. At 1.5 feet per cubit, it was 15 feet in diameter and 7.5 feet high. Although it was probably rounded around the edges, we will assume that it had the maximum possible volume for these dimensions, the shape of a cylinder. The volume of a cylinder is calculated by the formula:

Volume   = π *   (Radius squared)   *   Height

1325 cubic ft   = 3.14 *   (7.5 ^ 2)   *   7.5

There are about 6.23 gallons in a cubic foot, so the molten sea could hold a maximum of 1325 * 6.23 = 8,255 gallons, if 1 Kings 7:23 and 2 Chronicles 4:2 are correct. Since the walls of the sea were several inches thick, the inside of the sea might have been even smaller than this, if these measurements were made on the outside.

(continued on next page)

1 Kings 7:26 says that the sea had a capacity of 2,000 "baths"; this contradicts the dimensions reported in 1 Kings 7:23. 2 Chronicles 4:5 claims that the sea had a capacity of 3,000 "baths"; this contradicts the dimensions reported in 1 Chronicles 4:2.

The Hebrew word "bath" means something very different from the modern English word "bath". A Hebrew "bath" was a volume measurement in the same sense that the modern words "liter" or "gallon" represent volume measurements. The Scofield Reference Bible and Young's Concordance say that a "bath" was 8 gallons. Webster's New World Dictionary, Second Edition, says it was 6-10 gallons.

Taking the lowest of these, 6 gallons, still means that 1 Kings 7:26 claims that the sea held 2000 * 6 = 12,000 gallons. Since the maximum possible volume of the sea is about 8,255 gallons, 1 Kings 7:26 overstates its volume by at least 3,500 gallons, or 42%.

2 Chronicles 4:5 claims that the sea contained 3,000 * 6 = 18,000 gallons. Since the maximum possible volume of the sea is about 8,255 gallons, 2 Chronicles overstates its volume by at least 9,500 gallons, or 115%.

If a "bath" was larger than 6 gallons, these overstatements in Kings and Chronicles would have been mathematically wrong by even greater amounts.

The Molten Sea [8]

How Tall Were The Pillars In Front Of The Jerusalem Temple?

2 Chronicles 3:15 says, "He [Solomon] made before the house [the temple of the Lord] two pillars of thirty and five cubits high". One cubit was about 18 inches, so Chronicles is claiming that the pillars were each about 53 feet high.

But 1 Kings 7:15 says, "He cast two pillars of brass, of eighteen cubits high apiece". This is supported by Jeremiah 52:21, which says, "Concerning the pillars, the height of one pillar was eighteen cubits". 18 * 1.5 = 27 feet. So Kings and Jeremiah claim that the pillars were each about 27 feet high.

This is significant because Christian conservatives believe that Kings and Chronicles were both written almost entirely before the Temple was destroyed in 586 BCE, making them eyewitness historical accounts. Eyewitnesses could disagree by a small amount (although the Bible claims to be a perfect book and perfect eyewitnesses could not disagree). But eyewitnesses would not mistake a 50+ foot column for one half that size.

* * *

How Tall Were The Chapiters On The Jerusalem Temple?

Each of the two temple pillars had a "chapiter", or "capital" on top of it. These would have been similar to the crowns or scrollwork that you can see on the tops of Corinthian or Roman columns on some modern buildings, although they may have been much more ornate.

Jeremiah 52:21-22 describes the pillars in front of God's temple in Jerusalem, "And concerning the pillars, the height of one pillar was eighteen cubits; and a fillet of twelve cubits did compass it; and the thickness thereof was four fingers: it was hollow. And a chapiter of brass was upon it; and the height of one chapiter was **five cubits**, with network and pomegranates upon the chapiters round about, all of brass [some translations say "bronze"]. The second pillar also and the pomegranates were like unto these".

Jeremiah's claim is supported by 2 Chronicles 3:15, which says, "The chapiter that was on the top of each of them was **five cubits**".

But 2 Kings 25:17 says, "The height of the one pillar was eighteen cubits, and the chapiter upon it was brass, and the height of the chapiter **three cubits**; and the wreathen work, and pomegranates upon the chapiter round about, all of brass, and like unto these had the second pillar with wreathen work".

Notes

General Notes:

• All Bible quotes are from the King James Bible unless otherwise stated, because that translation is the most widely accepted one among Christian conservatives. When modern translations varied from the King James in ways that could effect the interpretation of mathematically relevant information, I added a quote or clarification from a modern translation, or a brief amplification in brackets [ ].

• Quotes from the "New American Standard Bible" are from the New American Standard Bible, copyright 1960, 1962, 1963, 1968 and 1971 by the Lockman Foundation.

• Quotes from the "Revised Standard Bible" are from The Holy Bible Containing The Old And New Testaments: Revised Standard Version, copyright 1946 and 1952 by William Collins Sons & Co, Ltd.

• Quotes from the "Moffatt Bible" are from The Holy Bible Containing The Old And New Testaments: A New Translation by James Moffatt, published in 1922.

• Quotes from the "Weymouth Bible" are from The New Testament In Modern Speech by R.F. Weymouth, published in 1912.

• I used Young's Analytical Concordance to determine which Hebrew or Greek word was used in a particular passage and how to transliterate it into the English alphabet. Young's Concordance was first published by Robert Young in 1879. Many editions of it are still in print.

• This book uses BCE, "Before the Common Era" and CE, "Common Era" instead of BC and AD, because the Bible says that Jesus was born during the reign of Herod, who died in 4 BCE, leading to the atheistically gratifying, but theologically inconsistent, conclusion that Jesus was born at least 4 years "Before Christ". For more details, please refer to "Dating the First Christmas (Christ-mass) is a Mess" in Chapter 2.

• Why do I capitalize "God", but not pronouns related to God, such as "he" or "him"? Because that is the way that my grammar book (The Chicago Manual of Style, 15th edition) says to do it.

Chapter 1 - Jesus' Math Mistakes

1 - Eusebius' Ecclesiastical History, Book 6, Chapter 8, commends Origen's self-castration as an act of superior faith and says that other Christians greatly admired him for it.

2 - This quote comes from Caesar and Christ, by Will Durant, page 659. Durant is quoting Eusebius' book, Life, 2:63:70

3 - Edward Gibbon, History of Christianity, pages 513-516, describes the Trinitarian Christian Roman Emperor Theodosius' persecution of non-Trinitarian Christians who were Arian, Manichean or Priscillian. Some were executed. Others were exiled and their property confiscated by the church; the rest were forcibly converted to Catholicism.

4 - There are at least 3 court cases where the judge ruled that thousands of people in the Bible Belt who drank polluted water were harmed by it and were entitled to monetary damages: Owens v Monsanto, Abernathy v Monsanto and Tolbert v Monsanto.

(continued on next page)

Chapter 2 - Math Mistakes About Jesus

1. Will Durant, Caesar and Christ, page 558.

2. Edwin and Alice Count, 4000 Years of Christmas, page 22, state that the Yuletide feast was originally for the heathen god Frey, and that the Yule log and Christmas tree originated as heathen religious practices in ancient Britain and Germany.

3. Will Durant, Caesar and Christ, page 558.

4. Will Durant, Caesar and Christ, page 558.

5. Josh McDowell, A Ready Defense, page 129, claims that the author of Matthew was actually combining the "prophecies" of Zechariah 11:12-13 and Jeremiah chapter 32. W Arndt, Does the Bible Contradict Itself?, pages 51-53, makes a similar claim. This overlooks the obvious facts that (a) Matthew 27:9-10 does not mention Zechariah, (b) both of these "prophecies" are reported in past tense as things that have already happened, not things that will happen, and, (c) neither of them mentions the Messiah/Christ,.

6. John Haley, Alleged Discrepancies in the Bible, originally published in 1881. It has been reprinted several times and is still in print. This quote is on page 153 of my 1881 copy of this book and on page 154 of a later printing.

7. This quote comes from page 33 of The Real Messiah, published by the National Conference of Synagogue Youth, in 1973.

8. The claim that Jesus' burial fulfilled the "prophecy" in Isaiah 53:9 is so widespread that it is difficult to find a commentator on Matthew or on Messianic prophecy that does not mention it. Examples include, but are by no means limited to, The Scofield Reference Bible's cross-reference on Matthew 27:60 and Strong's Exhaustive Concordance's Appendix "Prophecies of the Messiah Fulfilled in Jesus Christ".

Chapter 3 - "Historical" Math Mistakes

1. In Matthew 7:9-11, Jesus promised, "What man is there of you, whom if his son ask bread, will he give him a stone? Or if he ask a fish, will he give him a serpent? If ye then, being evil, know how to give good gifts unto your children, how much more shall your Father which is in heaven give good things to them that ask him?" In Numbers 11:4-5, the Hebrews asked for fish, "The children of Israel also wept again and said, Who shall give us flesh to eat? We remember the fish, which we did eat in Egypt freely". God's children asked for fish, but their Heavenly Father gave them poisoned birds.

2. This illustration of the Ark of the Covenant is from page 11 of Smith's Bible Dictionary, published in 1910 by William Smith, LL.D. According to the Bible, the Ark had to occasionally be moved during the Hebrews' nomadic period, from the time of Moses to David, because worship was centered around a movable "Tabernacle", a large tent. After Solomon built the Jerusalem Temple, the Ark was no longer moved because it stayed permanently in the "Holy of Holies", where only the High Priest was allowed to see it.

(continued on next page)

3. This illustration of the Old Testament altar is from Smith's Bible Dictionary. In earlier times, the altar was made of rough stones, which would have taken longer to burn the sacrifices than altar in the illustration, which was made of metal and had a grate to hold the animal over the fire. Whether it was made of rock or metal, it was always the same size: a square 5 cubits on each side.

4. The Scofield Reference Bible's comments on 1 Samuel Chapter 2 say that God called Samuel in 1165 BCE. Its comments on 1 Samuel Chapter 10 say that Samuel anointed Saul as king in 1095 BCE. 1165 - 1095 = 70 years.

5. The Anchor Bible: Ezra Nehemiah, by Jacob M Myers. This is part of a series of Bible commentaries published by Doubleday & Company in 1965. Myers notes on pages 4-5 that many ancient manuscripts note this math error in their margins, and in a few cases the in text itself.

Chapter 4 - Sexual Math Mistakes

1. Clergy have been sexually abusing children for a very long time. One good book on the subject is Betrayal of Trust: Clergy Abuse of Children, by Annie Laurie Gaylor, published in 1988. It is currently out of print, but hardcopies can be purchased from online bookstores. The entire book is available online for free at http://www.ffrf.org/legacy/books/betrayal.

2. Nobody has even one of the original manuscripts of the 66 books of the Bible. If they ever existed, all have been lost. The copies that have survived until modern times were made hundreds and in some cases over a thousand years after the "originals" supposedly were written, and disagree with each other in literally hundreds of thousands of ways. This begs the obvious questions: (A) Why did God let the originals get lost? (B) Why did God inspire authors to write perfect originals but did not inspire copyists to make perfect copies?

Chapter 6 - Scientific And Geographical Math Mistakes

1. The Red Limit, by Timothy Ferris, is an excellent book that describes the techniques that astronomers use to measure the distances to stars and galaxies, and the millions of man-hours that it took to develop and calibrate those techniques.

2. Christ in Egypt: The Horus-Jesus Connection, by D.M. Murdock, pages 200-201.

3. The Christ Conspiracy: The Greatest Story Ever Sold, by Acharya S, pages 109-115.

4. The Christ Conspiracy: The Greatest Story Ever Sold, by Acharya S, pages 109-115.

5. This quote comes from Encyclopedia Britannica, Volume 28 (1952), page 126.

6. History Of The Warfare Of Science With Theology In Christendom, by Andrew D White, Volume 1, pages 126-128.

7. History of the Warfare of Science With Theology In Christendom, pages 364-372

8. Although no contemporary drawings of the Molten Sea have survived, this drawing matches the Bible's description. It is from Smith's Bible Dictionary, page 33.

Appendix 1

Jesus Paid For Everyone's Sins With Just One Very Bad Day

Jesus paid for our sins with just one very bad day. Anyone who has worked in hospitals has seen people enduring worse suffering every day, for weeks and years. Although most of these human sufferers did not choose to suffer, history contains millions examples of people, such as soldiers, firefighters and law enforcement officers, who willingly risked their lives and health in the line of duty. Many of these were horribly wounded and lived for decades in intractable, intense and constant pain.

Let's look at the mathematics of Jesus' sacrifice. The Bible says that Jesus was arrested after dark on Thursday and died about 3 PM on Friday, that much of that time was spent in travel and interrogation, and that the torture did not start until well after midnight. But for simplicity's sake, let's assume it was one entire 24-hour day.

If we assume that the world is about 6,000 years old (not billions of years old like those wicked evolutionists), and that the average population of the world during that time was 500 million, you get:

$$6,000 \text{ years } \times \ 365 \text{ days per year } \times \ 500,000,000 =$$
$$1,095,000,000,000,000 \text{ person-days}$$

That is about 1 quadrillion person-days. Since every one of those person-days was lived by a depraved sinner, Jesus had to pay the penalty for them all in a single day. There are 86,400 seconds in a day.

$$1,095,000,000,000,000 \ / \ 86,400 \ = 12,673,611,111$$

That is about 12 billion human sin-days paid for with each second of Jesus' very bad day. That is 1/12 of one nanosecond per human sin-day. A nanosecond is one billionth of a second, the amount of time it takes a beam of light to travel 18 inches. Assuming that the average person lived 40 years (14,600 days), that's less than 1,217 nanoseconds of atonement per life, or about one million sinful human lives atoned for in each second in Jesus' one very bad day.

Of course, most of humanity never believed in Jehovah or Jesus, so they're burning in hell right now. So maybe it would be more realistic to apply this calculation only to those who are "saved".

(continued on next page)

The Bible does not provide much information on how many people have been (or are going to be) actually "saved". History does not provide much help either, because not only do census records not go back very far, but "Not every one that saith unto me, Lord, Lord, shall enter into the kingdom of heaven; but he that doeth the will of my Father which is in heaven" (Matt 7:21), and some countries, like the United States, do not collect religious data in their censuses. Since "strait is the gate, and narrow is the way, which leadeth unto life, and few there be that find it" (Matthew 7:14), we can assume that no more than 1% of people who have ever lived are actually "saved". This figure will certainly gratify Christian fundamentalists.

So our 1,217 nanoseconds of atonement per sinner becomes 121.7 microseconds per sinner, or about nine thousand sinners ushered through the pearly gates for each second of Jesus' one very bad day. For Jesus' investment of 121.7 microseconds saving one of us, we are each expected to give our whole lives to him.

Let's calculate the return on this investment. Since "saved" people will be singing Jesus' praises in Heaven forever, this is an infinite return on a finite investment.

So let's calculate the return on Jesus investment in just earthly days, since we're supposed to serve Jesus every day. Assuming that the average person lived 40 years after getting saved:

40 years   x   365 days per year   x   24 hours per day   x   3600 seconds per hour   =
1,261,440,000 seconds (about 1 billion seconds)

1,261,440,000 seconds   x   1 million   =   1,261,440,000,000,000 microseconds

1,261,440,000,000,000 microseconds divided by 121.7 microseconds
=   103,651,602,300,000 %

Jesus is getting a very admirable return on his investment of one very bad day, in terms of devotion, worship and praise from his followers.

Blind Faith

Bible believers often say that God does not expect his followers to have "blind faith". Let the Bible speak for itself.

• John 20:29, "Jesus saith unto him, Thomas, because thou hast seen me, thou hast believed, blessed are they that have not seen, and yet have believed"

• 2 Corinthians 4:18, "We look not at the things which are seen, but at the things which are not seen, for the things which are seen are temporal; but the things which are not seen are eternal"

• 2 Corinthians 5:7, "For we walk by faith, not by sight"

• Hebrews 11:1, "Now faith is the substance of things hoped for, the evidence of things not seen"

• Hebrews 11:3, "Through faith we understand that the worlds were framed by the word of God, so that things which are seen were not made of things which do appear"

• Romans 8:24-25, "We are saved by hope, but hope that is seen is not hope, for what a man seeth, why doth he yet hope for? But if we hope for that we see not, then do we with patience wait for it"

• Exodus 33:20, "no man see me [God] and live"

• John 1:18, "no man hath seen God at any time"

• 1 Timothy 6:15-16, "King of kings ... whom no man hath seen nor can see"

• Isaiah 64:4, "For since the beginning of the world men have not heard, nor perceived by the ear, neither hath the eye seen, O God, beside thee, what he hath prepared for him that waiteth for him". See also 1 Corinthians 2:9.

• 1 Timothy 1:17, "Unto the King eternal, immortal, invisible, the only wise God, be honour and glory for ever and ever. Amen"

• Galatians 3:11 & Hebrews 10:38, "The just shall live by faith"

• Luke 17:20-21, "The kingdom of God cometh not with observation. Neither shall they say, Lo here! or, lo there! for, behold, the kingdom of God is within you"

• Matt 11:25-26, "Jesus ... said, I thank thee, O Father ... because thou hast hid these things from the wise and prudent, and hast revealed them unto babes"

• 1 Corinthians 4:10, "We are fools for Christ's sake"

• 1 Corinthians 3:18-19, "If any man among you seemeth to be wise in this world, let him become a fool, that he may be wise. For the wisdom of this world is foolishness with God"

• 1 Corinthians 1:27, "God hath chosen the foolish things of the world to confound the wise"

Verse(s)	Page	Verse(s)	Page
Acts 1:13	39	2 Chronicles 11:13-14	67
Acts 2:22-23	10	2 Chronicles 14:8	64, 67
Acts 2:44-45	4	2 Chronicles 15:2	67
Acts 4:36	67	2 Chronicles 15:8-9	67
Acts 5:1-10	19	2 Chronicles 16:1	68
Acts 5:16	89	2 Chronicles 16:2-6	68
Acts 5:34-40	80	2 Chronicles 18:18-22	83
Acts 8:32-35	38	2 Chronicles 18:18-22	89
Acts 9:36-41	84	2 Chronicles 21:9-11	83
Acts 13:18	66	2 Chronicles 22:2	68
Acts 13:20	45, 66	2 Chronicles 25:5	67
Acts 13:21	66	2 Chronicles 26:16-21	60
Acts 13:39	92	2 Chronicles 28:5-8	69
Acts 16:16-18	89	2 Chronicles 31:1	67
Acts 19:12	89	2 Chronicles 315	110
Acts 20:9-12	20, 84	2 Chronicles 33:11-20	87
Acts 22:3	80	2 Chronicles 33:12	87
Amos 7:3	95	2 Chronicles 33:13	87
Amos 7:6	95	2 Chronicles 34:32	67
1 Chronicles 1:32	80	2 Chronicles 34:9	67
1 Chronicles 2:13-15	64	2 Chronicles 35:20-27	87
1 Chronicles 3:10-16	28	2 Chronicles 36:18	56
1 Chronicles 16:30	102	Colossians 2:9	1, 21, 27, 34
1 Chronicles 20:3	93	Colossians 3:20	93
1 Chronicles Chapter 21	65	1 Corinthians 1:27	116
1 Chronicles 21:5	64	1 Corinthians 3:18-19	116
1 Chronicles 21:6	64	1 Corinthians 3:3-7	16
1 Chronicles 22:8	7	1 Corinthians 4:10	116
2 Chronicles 1:11	67	1 Corinthians 5:5	89
2 Chronicles 3:15	110	1 Corinthians 5:5	95
2 Chronicles 4:2-5	108	1 Corinthians 6:16	77
2 Chronicles 5:10	82	1 Corinthians 7:29	4
2 Chronicles 5:9	56	1 Corinthians 10:10-17	16
2 Chronicles 11:12	67	1 Corinthians 10:13	34,79,83
2 Chronicles 11:13	67	1 Corinthians 10:20-21	89

Verse(s)	Page	Verse(s)	Page
1 Corinthians 11:18-19	16	Deuteronomy 20:16-17	12, 19, 54, 57, 58, 83
1 Corinthians 11:29-30	95		
1 Corinthians 13:4	94	Deuteronomy 21:22	103
1 Corinthians 14:34-35	5, 76	Deuteronomy 22:16-17	33
1 Corinthians 15:3-6	41	Deuteronomy 22:22	79
1 Corinthians 15:17-19	40	Deuteronomy 23:3	97
2 Corinthians 4:18	116	Deuteronomy 24:16	86, 95
2 Corinthians 5:7	44, 116	Deuteronomy 28:15-68	95
2 Corinthians 6:18	95	Deuteronomy 28:28	47
2 Corinthians 11:14	89	Deuteronomy 29:5	66
2 Corinthians 11:25	84	Deuteronomy 31:1-2	63
Daniel 12:2	97	Deuteronomy 31:4	57
Deuteronomy 2:30-34	55, 57	Deuteronomy 34:1-6	7
Deuteronomy 3:1-6	57	Deuteronomy 34:7	63
Deuteronomy 3:3-6	55	Ecclesiastes 1:4	96
Deuteronomy 3:6	55	Ecclesiastes 7:20	85
Deuteronomy 4:24	94	Ecclesiastes 9:5	97
Deuteronomy Chapter 5	82	Ephesians 6:11	89
Deuteronomy 5:17	54, 83, 94	Ephesians 4:3-6	16
Deuteronomy 5:18	79	Ephesians 5:18	13
Deuteronomy 5:9	94	Ephesians 5:18	22
Deuteronomy 6:2	95	Esther 4:3	88
Deuteronomy 6:13	83, 95	Esther 4:14	88
Deuteronomy 6:16	89	Esther 4:16	88
Deuteronomy 6:24	95	Esther 6:4	103
Deuteronomy 7:1-2	19, 55, 83	Esther 7:9-10	103
Deuteronomy 7:15	107	Esther 8:7	103
Deuteronomy 8:19-20	95	Esther 9:14	103
Deuteronomy 10:20	83	Exodus 1:1-5	63
Deuteronomy 12:27	61	Exodus 1:15-20	34
Deuteronomy 13:6-10	19	Exodus 1:5	74
Deuteronomy 17:17	75	Exodus 2:8	27
Deuteronomy 18:13	95	Exodus 4:11	18
Deuteronomy 18:20	19	Exodus 6:14-25	74
Deuteronomy 18:22	2, 9	Exodus 6:16-18	52

Verse(s)	Page	Verse(s)	Page
Exodus 6:20	52	Exodus 34:27-28	82
Exodus 7:7	52	Exodus 34:28	82
Exodus Chapters 11-12	46	Exodus Chapter 38	61
Exodus 12:29	96	Exodus 38:26	55, 60
Exodus 12:37	74	Ezekiel 14:9	90
Exodus 12:40-41	52	Ezekiel 16:38	95
Exodus 13:13	60	Ezekiel 23:25-26	95
Exodus 13:2-15	60	Ezekiel 33:12-13	85
Exodus 17:14	86	Ezra 1:11	71
Exodus 17:8	86	Ezra 1:1-4	70
Exodus 17:8-14	19	Ezra 1:1-8	70
Exodus 19:16	105	Ezra 1:5	67
Exodus Chapter 20	82	Ezra 1:7-11	71
Exodus 20:13	54, 83, 94	Ezra 1:9	71
Exodus 20:14	79	Ezra Chapter 2	65, 72
Exodus 20:5	94	Ezra 2:68-69	71
Exodus 22:24	95	Ezra Chapters 2-3	70
Exodus 29:18	60	Ezra 3:2-8	70
Exodus 30:11-12	65	Ezra 3:7	70
Exodus 32:12-14	95	Ezra 3:8	70
Exodus 32:19	82	Ezra Chapter 4	70
Exodus 32:27-28	7	Ezra 4:1	67
Exodus 32:27-35	95	Ezra 4:24	70
Exodus 33:20	116	Ezra 4:5	70
Exodus 34:1	82	Ezra 4:6	70
Exodus 34:12	82	Ezra 5:2	70
Exodus 34:14	82, 94	Ezra 5:2-7	70
Exodus 34:17	82	Ezra 5:5-6:15	70
Exodus 34:18	82	Ezra 5:6-8	70
Exodus 34:19	82	Ezra 6:15	70
Exodus 34:20	60	Ezra 6:7-14	70
Exodus 34:21	82	Ezra Chapter 7	70
Exodus 34:22	82	Ezra Chapter 8	70
Exodus 34:23	82	Ezra 9:1	58
Exodus 34:25-26	82	Galatians 1:8-9	19

Verse(s)	Page	Verse(s)	Page
Galatians 3:11	116	Genesis 11:32	49
Galatians 3:13	95	Genesis Chapters 15-17	48
Galatians 3:16-17	52	Genesis 15:16	74
Galatians 4:22	80	Genesis 16:1-6	80
Genesis 1:6-8	101	Genesis 19:4-8	85
Genesis 1:14-15	101	Genesis 21:1-5	80
Genesis 1:20-25	101	Genesis 21:5	49
Genesis 1:27	101	Genesis 22:1	12
Genesis 1:31	93	Genesis 22:1-13	34
Genesis 2:17	94	Genesis 22:18	52, 93
Genesis 2:19	101	Genesis 23:1	48, 52
Genesis 2:24	77	Genesis 25:1-2	48, 80
Genesis 2:7	101	Genesis 25:26	52
Genesis 3 Chapter	93	Genesis 25:7	48, 49
Genesis 5:23-24	84	Genesis 26:4	93
Genesis 5:32	49	Genesis 29:32 - 30:1	32
Genesis 6:2	89	Genesis 35:28	49
Genesis 6:5	46	Genesis 35:28-29	52
Genesis 6:6-7	95	Genesis 36:31	45
Genesis 6:9	85	Genesis 37:2	78
Genesis Chapter 7	46	Genesis 37:2-3	78
Genesis 7:11	49	Genesis 40:19-23	103
Genesis 7:21-23	46	Genesis 41:43	78
Genesis 9:1-16	50	Genesis 41:46	78
Genesis 9:6	50	Genesis 44:20	78
Genesis 9:29	49	Genesis 44:22-34	78
Genesis 11:10-11	49	Genesis 45:6-11	78
Genesis 11:10-13	49	Genesis Chapter 46	78
Genesis 11:10-32	49	Genesis 46:21	78
Genesis 11:14-17	49	Genesis 46:8-11	52
Genesis 11:16-29	49	Genesis 47:9	52
Genesis 11:18-21	49	Genesis 48:5	63
Genesis 11:20-23	49	Genesis 49:3-28	63
Genesis 11:22-25	49	Hebrews 2:18	34
Genesis 11:24-26	49	Hebrews 2:3-4	11

Index Of Bible References

Verse(s)	Page	Verse(s)	Page
Hebrews 4:15	6, 34, 83	Jeremiah 23:5	28
Hebrews 5:5-6	25	Jeremiah 31:15	32
Hebrews 6:18	90	Jeremiah 31:16-17	32
Hebrews 9:3	56	Jeremiah 32:8-10	35
Hebrews 9:4	56	Jeremiah 36:30	29
Hebrews 9:7	84	Jeremiah 52:21	110
Hebrews 9:26	84	Jeremiah 52:21-22	110
Hebrews 9:27	39, 84	Jeremiah 52:28-30	68
Hebrews 9:28	84	Job Chapters 1-2	89
Hebrews 10:38	116	Job 7:9	97
Hebrews 11:1	44, 116	Job 9:6	103
Hebrews 11:11-12	48	Job 26:7	103
Hebrews 11:13	116	Job 28:26	105
Hebrews 11:5	84	Job 37:3	105
Hebrews 12:26-27	84	Job 38:25	105
Hebrews 13:8	27	Job 38:35	105
Isaiah 1:18	87	Job 38:4-6	103
Isaiah 7:14	27	1 John 1:7	92
Isaiah 7:15-16	27	1 John 1:9	92
Isaiah 9:6-7	29	1 John 4:18	83
Isaiah 22:23-25	103	1 John 5:7	21
Isaiah 26:14	97	John 1:1	1, 20, 95
Isaiah 40:8	96	John 1:1-3	21
Isaiah 45:25	87	John 1:3	1
Isaiah 53:7	38	John 1:17	45
Isaiah 53:9	40	John 1:18	116
Isaiah 64:4	116	John 1:19	67
Isaiah 65:17	96	John 2:1-11	13
James 1:4	83	John 2:23	11
James 1:13	12, 34, 89	John 3:16	93
James 1:27	59	John 3:18	19
James 5:14-15	106	John 3:2	11
James 5:17	83	John 4:44	25
Jeremiah 17:4	97	John 4:48-54	11
Jeremiah 19:9	12, 83	John 5:26-27	21

Verse(s)	Page	Verse(s)	Page
John 6:2	11	John 18:34	38
John 6:5-6	12	John 18:36	38
John 6:14	11	John 18:37	38
John 6:26	10	John 19:11	38
John 6:64-71	9	John 19:14-16	43
John 7:19	45	John 19:26-27	38
John 7:31	11	John 19:30	38
John 8:24	20	John 19:38-42	40
John 8:44	90	John 20:12-13	43
John 10:30	20, 21, 27, 34, 95	John 20:17	3
John 10:41-42	11	John 20:19-26	42
John 11:1-44	34	John 20:29	44, 98, 116
John 11:43-44	84	John 20:30	11
John 11:45	11	Jonah 1:17	2
John 12:1-7	43	Jonah 3:10	95
John 12:17-18	11	Jonah 4:2	95
John 12:25	96	Joshua 2:3-4	34
John 12:37	10	Joshua 8:29	103
John 12:47-49	21	Joshua 8:32	45
John 13:18	25	Joshua 10:12-13	102
John 14:6	90	Joshua 10:12-14	104
John 14:9	1, 21	Joshua 10:26	103
John 14:12	20	Joshua Chapters 10-11	58
John 14:13-14	14, 106	Joshua Chapters 10-12	55
John 14:26	16	Joshua 11:14-15	57
John 14:28	21	Joshua 11:15	58
John 15:24-25	25	Joshua 11:23	58
John 15:26	16	Joshua 13:1-5	58
John 16:13-15	15	Joshua 14:7-10	45, 66
John 17:11	16	Joshua 15:21-32	62
John 17:12	9	Joshua 15:33-36	62
John 17:21-23	16	Joshua 18:21-25	32
John 18:17-27	8	Joshua 19:32-36	32
John 18:20-21	38	Joshua 21:43	58
John 18:23	38	Joshua 24:29	7, 45

Verse(s)	Page	Verse(s)	Page
Jude 6	89	1 Kings 10:16-36	8
Jude 9	7	1 Kings 11:3	75
Judges 1:9	69	1 Kings 11:11-13	67
Judges 1:34	57	1 Kings 11:15-16	93
Judges 2:17-18	95	1 Kings 12:21	67
Judges 3:1-5	58	1 Kings 12:23	67
Judges 3:8-11	66	1 Kings 14:16	83
Judges 3:14	66	1 Kings 15:5	93
Judges 3:30	66	1 Kings 16:6-8	68
Judges 3:31	66	1 Kings 16:9-12	68
Judges 4:3	66	1 Kings 19:11	18
Judges 4:4	25	1 Kings 22:20-23	83, 89
Judges 4:17-22	91	2 Kings 2:11	84
Judges 4:24	25	2 Kings 4:1-7	59
Judges 5:31	66	2 Kings 4:18-37	84
Judges 6:1	66	2 Kings 8:26	68
Judges 6:1-6	57	2 Kings 8:9	56
Judges 8:28	66	2 Kings Chapter 10	91
Judges 9:22	66	2 Kings 10:18-19	91
Judges 10:2	66	2 Kings 10:24-25	91
Judges 10:3	66	2 Kings 10:30	91
Judges 10:8	66	2 Kings 15:30	27
Judges 12:14	66	2 Kings 16:5	69
Judges 12:7	66	2 Kings 16:9	27
Judges 12:8-10	66	2 Kings 17:6	27
Judges 12:11-12	66	2 Kings 19:35	46
Judges 13:1	66	2 Kings 23:25	87
Judges 15:20	66	2 Kings 23:26-27	87
Judges 16:31	66	2 Kings 23:28-30	87
1 Kings 2:11	66	2 Kings 24:2	87
1 Kings 3:13	25	2 Kings 24:3	87
1 Kings 6:1	66	2 Kings 24:14	68
1 Kings 7:15	110	2 Kings 25:17	110
1 Kings 7:23-26	108	Lamentations 2:20	83
1 Kings 8:9	82	Lamentations 4:10	83

Verse(s)	Page	Verse(s)	Page
Leviticus 1:11	60	Luke 7:11-15	84
Leviticus 1:14-17	61	Luke 7:21	89
Leviticus 1:6-9	60	Luke 7:48-49	20
Leviticus 1:7	61	Luke 8:2	89
Leviticus 1:7-8	60	Luke 8:25	18
Leviticus 1:8-9	61	Luke 8:26-36	89
Leviticus 1:9	60	Luke 9:26	4
Leviticus 4:27-34	60	Luke 9:27	4
Leviticus 4:6	60	Luke 9:38-42	89
Leviticus 5:1-7	60	Luke 10:18	105
Leviticus 5:2-7	60	Luke 11:14	89
Leviticus 6:2-7	60	Luke 11:24-26	89
Leviticus 10:1-2	60	Luke 11:29	10
Leviticus 10:16	60	Luke 11:29-30	2
Leviticus 15:25-30	60	Luke 12:10	18, 19, 92
Leviticus 17:1-5	60	Luke 12:7	1
Leviticus 22:21	60	Luke 13:11	89
Leviticus 26:18	95	Luke 17:20-21	116
Leviticus 26:26-30	95	Luke 18:20	79
Leviticus 27:2	76	Luke 21:33	96
Luke 1:5-6	85	Luke 22:34	8
Luke 1:32	29	Luke 22:56-58	8
Luke 2:1	65	Luke 22:67-69	38
Luke 2:1-9	100	Luke 22:70	38
Luke 2:2	31	Luke 23:3	38
Luke 2:4	32	Luke 23:28-31	38
Luke 3:31-33	32	Luke 23:34	38
Luke 4:1-13	6, 89	Luke 23:43	3, 38
Luke 4:5-7	6	Luke 23:46	38
Luke 4:24	25	Luke 23:50-53	40
Luke 4:28-30	34	Luke 24:4-7	43
Luke 4:33-36	89	Luke 24:9	41
Luke 4:41	89	Luke 24:33	41
Luke 5:18-25	20	Luke 24:33-39	42
Luke 6:17-18	89	Malachi 1:4	97

Verse(s)	Page		Verse(s)	Page
Mark 1:21-27	89		Matthew 2:1	30
Mark 1:32	89		Matthew 2:1-6	29
Mark 1:34-39	89		Matthew 2:16	30
Mark 2:5-11	20		Matthew 2:16-18	32
Mark 3:18	58		Matthew 2:22	31
Mark 3:28-30	18, 19		Matthew 4:1-10	89
Mark 3:29	92		Matthew 4:7	89
Mark 3:7-11	89		Matthew 4:24	89
Mark 5:1-13	89		Matthew 5:17	95
Mark 6:4	25		Matthew 5:18	24
Mark 6:13	89		Matthew 5:22	95
Mark 7:15-19	22		Matthew 5:32	12, 34, 79
Mark 7:25-30	89		Matthew 5:33-37	83
Mark 8:11-12	10		Matthew 5:48	1, 95
Mark 9:17-27	89		Matthew 6:9	95
Mark 10:11-12	73		Matthew 6:13	79
Mark 10:46-52	36		Matthew 6:14-15	19
Mark 13:31	96		Matthew 6:20	96
Mark 13:32	21		Matthew 6:27	17
Mark 14:1-8	43		Matthew 7:12	18
Mark 14:30	8		Matthew 7:14	114
Mark 14:62	38		Matthew 7:21	114
Mark 14:68-72	8		Matthew 8:16	89
Mark 15:2	38		Matthew 8:26	18
Mark 15:25	43		Matthew 8:28-34	89
Mark 15:37	38		Matthew 9:2-7	20
Mark 15:43-47	40		Matthew 9:32	89
Mark 16:14	41		Matthew 10:2-4	9
Mark 16:17	89		Matthew 10:4	58
Mark 16:17-18	23		Matthew 10:28	95
Matthew 1:2-6	32		Matthew 10:30	1
Matthew 1:5	97		Matthew 11:25-26	116
Matthew 1:6-11	28		Matthew 12:22	89
Matthew 1:17	28		Matthew 12:31-32	18, 19, 92
Matthew 1:23	27		Matthew 12:38-40	3, 10

Verse(s)	Page	Verse(s)	Page
Matthew 12:40	2	Matthew 27:52-53	39, 84
Matthew 12:43-45	89	Matthew 27:57-60	40
Matthew 13:17	85	Matthew 28:1-7	43
Matthew 13:57	25	Matthew 28:16-17	41
Matthew 15:11-17	22	Matthew 28:18	1, 18, 89
Matthew 15:22	89	Nahum 1:5	47
Matthew 16:4	2, 10	Nehemiah 11:35-36	67
Matthew 16:27	4	Nehemiah 11:4	67
Matthew 16:28	4	Nehemiah Chapter 7	65, 72
Matthew 17:15-18	89	Nehemiah 7:70-71	71
Matthew 18:8-9	5	Numbers 1:46	74
Matthew 18:19-20	14, 15	Numbers 3:4	60
Matthew 18:21-22	19	Numbers 3:40-43	74
Matthew 19:4-8	73	Numbers 4:15	60
Matthew 19:9	73	Numbers 11:1	95
Matthew 19:12	5	Numbers 11:31-32	53
Matthew 19:18	79	Numbers 11:33	53
Matthew 19:28	9	Numbers 13:2-15	63
Matthew 19:29	96	Numbers 15:27-27	60
Matthew 20:29-34	36	Numbers 16:49	46
Matthew 21:15-16	25	Numbers 18:6-8	60
Matthew 22:37	83	Numbers 18:6-8	97
Matthew 23:29	85	Numbers 21:2-3	58
Matthew 23:35	85	Numbers 21:3	7, 55
Matthew 24:35	96	Numbers 21:33-35	7, 54
Matthew 24:36-37	21	Numbers 23:19	95
Matthew 26:28	20	Numbers 25:1-9	46
Matthew 26:34	8	Numbers 26:38-40	78
Matthew 26:52	7, 93	Numbers 26:51	55, 74
Matthew 26:64	38	Numbers Chapter 31	57
Matthew 26:69-72	8	Numbers 31:1-2	59
Matthew 26:71-72	8	Numbers 31:6-35	7, 54, 55
Matthew 27:9-10	35	Numbers 31:14-18	59
Matthew 27:11	29, 38	Numbers 31:17	33
Matthew 27:50 3	8	Numbers 31:35	59

Verse(s)	Page	Verse(s)	Page
Numbers 32:11-13	74	Psalm 68:25	27
1 Peter 2:17	83	Psalm 75:3	47, 103
1 Peter 3:8	16	Psalm 77:18	105
1 Peter 3:18	84	Psalm 78:69	96
1 Peter 4:3	22	Psalm 79:1-5	95
1 Peter 5:8	89	Psalm 93:1	102, 103
2 Peter 2:4	89	Psalm 96:10	102
2 Peter 2:7-8	85	Psalm 97:4	105
2 Peter 2:9	83	Psalm 97:5	47
2 Peter 3:10	47	Psalm 103:2-3	106
2 Peter 3:10-13	96	Psalm 103:3	18, 92
Philippians 3:5	67	Psalm 103:8-9	97
Philippians 3:18-19	95	Psalm 104:5	96
Proverbs 4:10-11	17, 107	Psalm 111:9	96
Proverbs 4:20-22	17	Psalm 115:17	97
Proverbs 9:10-11	17	Psalm 135:7	105
Proverbs 10:12	92	Psalm 136	96
Proverbs 10:27	17, 107	Psalm 136:6	103
Proverbs 12:10	46, 47	Psalm 136:10	96
Proverbs 15:3	33	Psalm 137:2	103
Proverbs 23:29-32	13	Psalm 144:6	105
Proverbs 24:21	83	Psalm 145:16	46
Proverbs 30:19	27	Psalm 145:30	92
Psalm 6:5	97	Psalm 146:9	59
Psalm 18:14	105	Psalm 146:10	96
Psalm 18:20-24	85	Revelation 4:5	105
Psalm 24:1-2	103	Revelation 7:4-8	63
Psalm 25:7	87	Revelation 8:5	105
Psalm 30:5	97	Revelation 8:7	47
Psalm 33:7	103	Revelation 8:8-9	47
Psalm 33:8-9	102	Revelation 11:5	105
Psalm 55:23	107	Revelation 14:7	83
Psalm 58:10	55	Revelation 16:3	47
Psalm 68:5	59	Revelation 16:12	47
Psalm 68:17	69	Revelation 16:17-20	47

Verse(s)	Page	Verse(s)	Page
Revelation 16:18	105	1 Samuel 15:29	95
Revelation 20:12-15	1	1 Samuel 15:35	95
Revelation 20:14	20	1 Samuel 16:10-13	64
Revelation 21:8	90	1 Samuel 17:12-14	64
Romans 1:17	44	1 Samuel 18:20-27	93
Romans 3:10	85	1 Samuel 19:11-18	34
Romans 4:1-5	48	1 Samuel Chapter 22	55
Romans 8:24-25	116	1 Samuel 27:8-11	54, 55
Romans 9:11	54	1 Samuel 27:8-12	91, 93
Romans 10:5	45	1 Samuel 27:9	7
Romans 11:1	67	2 Samuel 3:2-5	75
Romans 12:16	16	2 Samuel 4:12	103
Romans 13:1-7	83	2 Samuel 5:4-5	66
Romans 15:5-6	16	2 Samuel 5:7-10	93
Romans 15:26	4	2 Samuel 5:7-9	7
Ruth 4:13-17	97	2 Samuel 6:6-7	56
1 Samuel 1:1	32, 97	2 Samuel 8:2	93
1 Samuel 1:1-28	25	2 Samuel 12:24	75
1 Samuel 1:20	97	2 Samuel 17:17-22	34
1 Samuel 2:30-31	95	2 Samuel 21:12	103
1 Samuel 3:20	25	2 Samuel Chapter 24	12, 46, 64, 83
1 Samuel 4:18	66	2 Samuel 24:1	65
1 Samuel 5:6-12	47	2 Samuel 24:9	64
1 Samuel 6:13-19	56	2 Samuel 24:10-15	65
1 Samuel 6:19	46	2 Samuel 24:16	95
1 Samuel 7:10-14	97	1 Thessalonians 4:3	93
1 Samuel 7:15	66, 97	1 Thessalonians 4:17	84
1 Samuel 7:9	97	2 Thessalonians 2:10-11	83
1 Samuel 9:15-10:1	45	2 Thessalonians 3:3	83
1 Samuel 15:11	95	1 Timothy 1:17	116
1 Samuel 15:2	12	1 Timothy 2:11-15	76
1 Samuel 15:2-3 19,	86	1 Timothy 3:3	22
1 Samuel 15:3	33	1 Timothy 3:4-5	73
1 Samuel 15:3-8	54, 55	1 Timothy 3:7	89
1 Samuel 15:7-9	86		

Verse(s)	Page
1 Timothy 3:8	13, 22
1 Timothy 4:1	89
1 Timothy 5:9-11	59
1 Timothy 6:15-16	116
2 Timothy 1:10	20
Titus 1:7-8	22
Titus 2:2-3	22
Titus 2:3	13
Titus 2:9	93
Zechariah 4:9	70
Zechariah 11:12-13	35
Zephaniah 1:18	95
Zephaniah 3:8	95

Subject Index

Subject	Page
Aaron	60
Abraham	48, 80
Addiction	34
Adultery, Inescapable	79
Ahaz	69
All	92
Altar, of God	60
Amalekites	86
Amorites	57
Andromeda Galaxy	99
Angels	43, 69
Animals, killing	46, 47
Apostles	41, 42
Apostles	9
Archelaus	31
Arian Controversy	21
Ark of the Covenant	56, 82
Baasha	68
Bartimaeus	36
Benjamin	78
Bethlehem	32, 100
Biostatistics	16
Blind men	36
Bruno, Giordano	102
Calvin, John	103
Canaanites	58
Cannibalism	12
Castration	4
Census	65, 72
Chariots	69
Chemical Dependency	22, 34
Christmas	30
Chronology, Genesis	48
Cities	62
Clement of Alexandria	30

Subject	Page
Cock Crowing	7
Commandments, Ten	82
Copernicus	102
Copying Errors	24
Creation of man	101
Crucifixion	38, 43
Cyrenius	31
Cyrus	70, 71
Darius	70
David	6, 25, 64, 5, 77, 85, 91, 93
Death	84
Deborah	25
Defiling yourself	22
Denominations, Church	16
Deportation	68
Devil	5, 89
Dionysus	30
Disciples, Twelve	42
Divorce	79
Double Standard	19
Drugs	23
Drunkenness	13, 22
Earth, destruction of	47
Earth, flat	5
Easter	1
Egypt	52
Eratosthenes	5
Esther	88
Eunuchs	4
Evil Spirits	89, 90
Fear of God	83
Flesh, one	77
Flood, Noah's	46
Forever	96

Subject	Page
Forgiveness	19, 87
Foundation of the Earth	103
Franklin, Benjamin	105
Frey	30
Galileo	102
Genealogy, Jesus	28
Genocide	33, 54, 59
Genocide	86, 94
Golden Rule	18
Grave, Jesus'	40
Hammurabi	24
Healing by faith	14, 15
Health	14, 15, 17
Heart surgery	106
Height, Human	17
Heliocentric Solar System	102
Herod	30, 32, 100
Holy Spirit	16
Horus	30
Hospitals	15
Hydrology	103
Immanuel	27
Isaac	48
Jacob	78
Jael	91
Jealousy	94, 95
Jehioakim	28
Jehu	6, 91
Jesse	64
Joseph	78
Joseph of Arimathea	40
Josephus, Antiquities	31
Joshua	6, 104
Josiah	87
Judah	62

Subject	Page
Judas Iscariot	9, 35
Judgement Day	3, 9
Julian Calendar	30
Justice	86
Keturah	80
King, of Israel	45
Law, Old Testament	24
Leah	32
Light Year	99
Lightning	105
Longevity	14, 17, 107
Luther, Martin	102
Lying	83, 89, 90, 91
Manasseh	87
Manna	56
Mark, Inspiration of	37
Mary	43
Medications	23
Mercy	86
Midian	57, 59
Mithras	30
Moon	104
Morality	86
Moses	6, 45, 52, 63, 82
Murder	54, 59
Mutilation	4
Nebuchadnezzar	68
Noah	46
Not	94
Ointment	43
Omnipotence	86
Orbit of Earth	102, 103
Origen of Alexandria	4
Orphans	59
Paul	80

Subject	Page
Pedophilia	34, 77
Penicillin	15
Peter	7
Pharaoh	78
Pi	108
Pillars of the Earth	103
Plagues	65
Poison	23
Pollution	23
Polygamy	75
Prayer	14, 15
Procreation	74
Prophecy, false	2, 3, 9
Prophet, honored	25
Prostitution	93
Quail	53
Quintillius Varus	31
Rachel	32, 78
Ramah	32
Repentance, of God	95
Resurrection	1, 2, 39, 40, 42, 43
Righteousness	85
Sacrifice for sins	95
Samuel	25
Satan	65
Saul	86
Sea, in Jerusalem Temple	108
Shealtiel	70
Signs	10, 11
Silver, 30 pieces	35
Sin, Inescapable	12, 34, 83
Slaughter of Innocents	32, 33
Sol Invictus	30

Subject	Page
Solomon	25
Solomon	67, 75, 77
Solstice	30
Stars	99, 100, 101
Substance Abuse	22, 34
Sun	104
Surgery	106
Sword	6
Temple, Jerusalem	66, 70, 71, 108, 110
Temptation by Jesus	12, 13
Temptation of Jesus	5, 34
Ten Commandments	82
Textual Analysis	24
Theodosius	21
Throne of David	29
Tomb of Jesus	40
Trial of Jesus	38
Tribes of Israel	63, 67
Truth	16
Twelve Apostles	41, 42
Unpardonable Sin	18, 19, 93
Virgin Birth	27
Virgins	57, 59
Wandering Jew	3
Widows	59
Wine	13
Wise Men	100
Wittenburg University	102
Women	76
Works	20
Yule	30
Zerubbabel	70